To Miles & Vanessa

FINDING ME FROM M.E.

By

Karen Podevyn

CONTENTS

MY PERSONAL (AND BLUNT) NOTE TO YOU

When I was first diagnosed with M.E. I found it incredibly hard to believe it. I struggled to accept that I was so ill. I certainly couldn't take in what the medical professionals were telling me - that there was no official treatment, no medical cure and that I should try to learn to 'manage' it. I especially hated that I was led to believe that I may even get worse. Everywhere I looked there were horror stories of people suffering for years, for decades, for the rest of their lives even!

I kept hoping that one day things would 'magically' get better. I hoped that the doctors would find something to help me. I was praying for a miracle cure, and I desperately wanted a 'quick fix'.

Everything was hard work and so for a long time I didn't even want to do the one thing I really needed to do if I had any chance of recovering, which was to commit to working on myself fully.

Here is what I will tell you, which I wish someone had told me. It's a bitter pill to swallow, I know, and it feels very blunt to say it like I am going to. But I believe it's necessary.

No one else will make you get better.

This is all down to **YOU**. It will take hard work and dedication. It will mean you stepping out of your comfort zone and trying different things (some of these things may be things that you have previously mocked). It will mean you doing a lot of inner work to find out exactly what your body is telling you. It will mean accepting that your body is actually trying to *protect* you (I know, that's a **really** tough one to accept) by putting you in a position where you can no longer do the things you may want to. You will have to learn how to say *no* to other people (and say yes to your own self-care).

There may be big things which need to change if you want to get truly better. In all honesty, these things may end up being too big for you to feel able to change initially. If you come to realise that your illness is due to you being in an abusive relationship, a job you hate, a toxic environment, a past you don't feel able to deal with or a highly stressful situation which you just don't feel able to change (yet), even though you know it's having such negative effects on you - then you are unlikely to get truly better unless you *do* change that situation. That's a difficult thing to deal with!

It may come as a shock to you to realise how ill a bad situation can make you. Of course, we all know what it feels like to be 'stressed' but we don't always realise, or accept, just how unwell we can become through it. It takes a very strong person to make massive changes in life. Even when we know that something may be harming us, it can be difficult to make the adjustments which are necessary to ensure we can live our best lives.

Throughout this book I advocate working on your mindset in a huge way. I truly believe that when you have the right mindset, you can tackle anything. I had to work *so* hard on my mindset, and the truth is, I still must work hard on it.

It can be easy to make excuses about why *you* personally can't get better or achieve something which someone else has done. Don't get me wrong, I've done this myself! I've looked at other people and told myself 'Well, it's alright for them because they weren't as unwell as me/ had better support/ could afford more than me/ (insert whatever excuse you choose here)'. But the truth of it is, people get through things even when all the odds are stacked against them. Looking further afield from M.E. people may have an accident and be told they will never walk again... but they do. People can be told they have terminal cancer and be given six months to live... but then go on to live for decades. People may be told that they will never amount to anything in life... then go on to great successes in life! Every day we can find stories of people who have achieved almost unbelievable things... and there is genuinely nothing stopping YOU being one of those people!

For me, it all starts with what you tell yourself! If you are reading this and making excuses about why you *won't* or *can't* get better, then the chances are that you won't get better. What you tell yourself is likely to become true. This isn't just me promoting positive thinking. You can think as positively as you like, but if you don't also put the work in on yourself, you can't truly hope to do better in life. Thinking positively is wonderful - but you must put the action in as well!

We live in such a fast-paced world; one where it can be so hard to switch off from. Ironically, we have more time saving devices and better technology than ever before... yet we are often more stressed than possibly ever before. Our fight and flight responses were designed to keep us safe from true dangers, yet they seem to be switched on for things as seemingly simple as replying to an email or even just watching TV nowadays! We live in an almost constant state of 'drama' and it is not doing our bodies or health any good whatsoever. If you are always tuning in to the news, or scrolling through a social media feed filled with drama, watching TV shows designed to be intense or even getting caught up in complaining about countless different things on a daily basis, is it any wonder that you may feel less than 100%, even without a serious illness thrown in?

To get better, you *must* become aware of what you are filling your mind with, because what you fill your mind with will actually correspond with what you fill your body with. Your mind and body are so connected and if your mind is filled with rubbish, the cells of your body will be too. You must **choose** to fill it with good stuff. That may mean stepping away from what is now considered to be the 'norm' with the things you get involved in. This will not be a bad thing!

Our bodies weren't designed to consume the types of food and drink we now consume daily. The amount of chemicals found in everyday foods is incomprehensible! Our bodies were designed to eat *real* food, without the addition of all the additives so many foods now have. When we are overloading our bodies with chemicals, we are simply poisoning ourselves. To improve your health, you must be willing to eat well! Again, this means stepping away from what society now deems to be normal in a lot of ways, and getting back to eating whole foods which provide us with real nutrition!

Healing isn't always easy. It's not a straight path. It can be messy, uncomfortable, and even painful. You will come up against things which you may rather not deal with. You may unearth issues from your past which you have tried hard to bury. You may have to cope with emotions which you quite simply don't want to process.

Deal with them. Stop burying them. Trust in the process and know that it is for your greater good. Be willing to seek help, possibly even professional help for this part! It will always be worth it. Doing the 'inner work' is what can make a big difference in your recovery. Also please accept that this isn't going to be a 'quick fix'. It probably won't just take a few months, or even years... it may be a lifetime of working on yourself! But it **is** worth it to live your best life!

M.E. is an horrific illness. It can strip you of so much - and it can be so easy to feel like giving up when you are told that there is no medical treatment or cure. But you **can** recover from it! Not everyone will unfortunately... but **you** can... **if** you are willing to do whatever it takes to find out what will work for you. **If** you can be strong enough to accept that your recovery is up to you and stop waiting for someone/something else to come along and fix you. **If** you are willing to be brutally honest with yourself, sit and work out what this illness is trying to *tell* you and then put the work into doing the things which *will* help you! This is your own personal journey and while all the things I am talking about in this book can help everyone, it may be one or all the things I suggest which make a big difference for **you**!

I genuinely believe that you can get better. I do not believe that you are destined to a life of pain and horrific symptoms. I do not believe that you should keep holding out hope for a 'cure', but that you should choose to do the work yourself which will help you to recover.

I know that when you choose to put yourself and your recovery first, you will see benefits. You may right now be wanting your 'old life' back, and you may be wondering how anyone with this condition can ever be able to talk about how they feel grateful for ever being ill... but I really believe that one day you may feel that gratitude yourself, and you may even end up with a better 'new life'. I know this to be true... because it is exactly what I have done. And as the saying goes... If I can do it, then so can you!

INTRODUCTION

In 2018 I got ill. Really ill. Life changingly ill. Almost overnight, my whole world was turned upside down from what I initially assumed was a simple chest infection. I had no idea that I would be diagnosed with something as life changing as M.E. I didn't even really understand what M.E. was or know that much about it. I assumed that you got 'tired' from it. I knew that it was serious, although I didn't really know why. I had no idea what it could do to you...and what it could do to those people in your life who loved you and must watch you struggle through it, while struggling themselves at the utter powerlessness of their own actions. During my illness, I tried to remain as positive as I could, and I used writing as a form of therapy. I chronicled a lot of what was going on via social media, as I thought that it was important to try and raise awareness of this debilitating illness. I knew that if I had not really understood about it, I would not be the only one. I wanted to show people that it was so much more than simply 'being tired'. I needed people to see that while you may see someone with this illness and they seem 'ok', you may have no idea how **not** ok they truly are. How difficult it is to simply try and appear ok for even a few minutes and what damage you can do to yourself just trying to do seemingly 'normal' things.

I was unsure whether I would ever get better. Unfortunately, you aren't always given much hope. I was told by the professionals that I should learn how to manage it, that I may never recover, and to prepare myself that I would possibly get worse. I was scared. I felt so young to get a diagnosis like this. I felt so vulnerable, suddenly so fragile. I was terrified at what my children were witnessing. I was working so hard on putting on a brave face and just the effort of doing that was completely exhausting me.

I decided that I would always remain hopeful, to the best of my ability. I did my research. I did things which I thought would help. I followed the advice I was initially given.

However, I didn't get better. I got worse. I gave up the things I was trying as I wasn't getting the results I wanted. I told myself that I had a good mindset, when the truth was, I was constantly lying to myself about what was really going on.

One week, everything changed. The worst week I had ever experienced occurred. As is often the case when bad things happen to people, it catapulted me into a new way of living. It was exactly what I needed to make me change my own life. I agreed to finally treat my recovery as a full-time job. I changed so many things and I fully committed to myself.

Within just a few weeks I was seeing differences. Big differences. We were all shocked; optimistic but staying cautious. Constantly panicking about whether I would relapse. I had to learn to let go of that fear if I wanted to move on.

Within six months the differences were incredible. I was pretty much symptom free. I hardly had any pain. My energy levels had hugely risen. I was out and about every day doing things like picking the kids up and taking them to various places. I was thinking more clearly. I didn't slur my speech. I was sleeping better. I had lost all the 3 stone plus I had put on since being poorly. I was walking, and tentatively started the Couch to 5K (C25K) regime and began jogging a bit again. I got a part time job in my dream place. My children told me that they had stopped worrying so much that I was dying.

I knew that I still had a long way to go, but I was so incredibly happy. My whole family were delighted.

While part of my recovery was not being on social media as much as I had been during my illness, I was still journaling part of my recovery on there and receiving so much support. I realised that the things I were doing were not just helpful for people with M.E. (as well as for people with Fibromyalgia and Long Covid) but could potentially help anybody, no matter what was going on in their lives. A few people suggested I should write a book. I loved the thought of that, as I had always enjoyed writing, so decided to give it a go.

I am writing this book in the hope that it can help even one person. Obviously, I would love to help people with M.E. as it's such an important thing for me to do. I appreciate that for anyone with M.E. this book may be hard going, because anything and everything can be hard going. When you are as ill as someone with M.E. you can never take anything for granted.

I also would love this book to help people *without* M.E. What I am writing about is not rocket science. I am unlikely to tell you anything which you won't have heard before. I will discuss things that you may scoff at. I will suggest things that you may have already tried and told yourself that they aren't for you. I may even say things which you disagree with. That's all fine. I hope that anyone who reads this can take even one thing from it which helps you change your own life for the better (even if it's in a small way). I know that a huge purpose in my life is to help others (I've realised that I must do that now without making myself ill) and so that is why I am writing this book. A good bit of advice I recently heard when reading/listening to anything like this, is to take whatever you need from it, and leave the rest! I hope that works for you!

The first part of this book covers my story. It's about me before I became unwell, me during my illness, and the week which changed everything.

The second part covers all the things which I have done to aid my personal recovery and goes into some detail about them. They are not in any special order, and I will never say that it is any one thing which has helped over another. I don't really know whether it was any particular thing which worked better than another, as I was so determined to get better that I committed to doing all of them. What I will say though, is that ultimately the **best** thing you can ever do for yourself is learn how to control your mindset. Once you have the right mindset and know *why* you are doing anything, it makes everything else easier. I'm not saying **easy**. Truth be told, I didn't find any of the changes I made to be easy at the start, but they became easier once I had purpose behind what I was doing, and I could see the results which I desired occurring.

The third part is a section which covers how I am now.

I truly hope that this book brings hope to other people with M.E. as well as maybe giving people without the illness some inspiration for changes they can make to help improve their own lives. I want this book to raise some more understanding of the illness too. We all must take responsibility for our own lives, although for a lot of reasons, we may not always do that. It can be easier to blame circumstances, other people, and even the past for what's going on and how we feel. The truth is, the more we take control of the things we do each day, the better our lives will be. Most of the things which I have done to help me in my own recovery can be done by anyone and can really make differences in your life.

This book is not a 'quick fix' book – because unfortunately there is no quick fix with M.E. I am not a doctor or medically trained in any way, so nothing in this book is designed to be any sort of professional medical advice. I would always urge anyone affected by this illness to seek professional medical advice. I will not go into any overly complicated, or scientific terms and explanations in here (because if I'm honest, they never really helped me get better, and they quite often left me feeling totally overwhelmed).

I hope that you enjoy reading this book, and I thank you for taking the time and using your precious energy to do it. I certainly know that time and energy should never be taken for granted and so appreciate that yours is going into reading this. I truly hope that you get some value from it.

PART 1
ME BEFORE M.E.

Have you ever looked at someone and wondered how they do it all? People used to say that about me before I got ill. The ironic thing is that when they said it to me, I didn't believe they were being serious. I always felt like I could, and *should*, be doing more. I was guilty of constantly comparing myself to others and thinking that everyone else was somehow 'better' at life than me. I pushed myself, took on more and more, felt guilty if I ever said no, didn't like to take proper rest or time out for myself... and eventually it all caught up with me and I truly believe it was a reason why I became so ill.

I was born to my amazing parents in 1981 in Bolton. I would love to say I was a dream baby, but apparently, I was a shocker! Whilst my baby and toddler years weren't too easy for my parents (or so the story goes!), I had calmed down and become the perfect child by the time I had got to school. Ok, maybe 'perfect' is pushing it... but this is my story, and I'm allowed one bit of poetic license, so this is it! I loved school and worked hard to get good grades. I wanted to please my teachers and my family so made sure that I always did my best. I didn't have a great deal of self-confidence or self-esteem from an early age unfortunately, and I used to wish that I could do better. I worried about what people thought of me and even when I was young, I was very self-critical. It makes me a bit sad to think about how mean I was to myself, even as a young girl.

I worked hard all through my educational years. When I was 13, I got my first job, delivering papers seven days a week from the local newsagent. I had a strong work ethic and believed even from being young, that if you were physically and mentally able to work, that you should do.

After school, I went on to sixth form, and then onto Manchester Metropolitan University, where I studied Food and Nutrition. Whilst I was at college and university, I had two jobs - one working at a local restaurant behind a bar, and another working at our local department store café. I absolutely loved those jobs... although it was sometimes hard working so much while being at university full time.

After university, I wasn't sure what to do. I knew I didn't want to do anything with my degree and so I stayed at my job in the café where I had been made a supervisor and considered entering their management programme.

Randomly, I heard an advert for the police one day and decided it would be a good idea to apply for that. I genuinely never had any yearning to join the police when I was younger. Clearly, I was meant to do it though. In hindsight, I realise that it was the desire to help people which propelled me to apply and join.

I had no idea what to expect and looking back I was a naïve 22-year-old who was suddenly thrust onto the streets of Greater Manchester. It was all a bit surreal. Sometimes I would heave a sigh of relief when chaos was reigning, and I would hear somebody shout 'the police are here'... but then I would realise that they meant me, which was quite scary!

I spent just over ten years in the police. It was amazing, scary, horrific, fun, exhausting, exhilarating, hard (sometimes really, *really* hard), occasionally boring... and a whole host of other things! I met some real characters, both colleagues and members of the public. I attended incidents which to this day still haunt me, experienced situations which made me laugh, and lots of things in between the two. Being in the police certainly gives you life experience in a way which other jobs never will. You see people at their worst, and that can be difficult to deal with. You must often put your own life on hold, while you help people pick up the pieces when they are dealing with the worst thing they may ever go through.

I spent a few years in uniform, on the response section, which meant I was dealing with daily jobs, including 999 emergency calls. One minute you could be sent to a shoplifter, the next a pub fight with weapons and horrific violence, the next to a domestic violence situation, then a traffic accident, a drink-driver, a work accident, a sudden death, giving death messages, and being stood on major crime scenes.

I then did a couple of different jobs within different units, before specialising in the Public Protection Unit. I was a domestic violence officer, so my day-to-day jobs dealt with victims and perpetrators of domestic violence, child abuse and sexual offences. It was a very intense role and one which can certainly come home with you in many ways.

While I was in the police, I met my most favourite person in the world, my now husband, James. We joined at the same time, and he initially worked on the following shifts to mine. We became friends, and our love story is my most favourite! We became a couple after some time, lived together for a while before getting engaged and then married. We both wanted children and although we devastatingly lost a couple of precious babies along the way, we were blessed to go on to have Jack and Isobel. James left the police after we had Jack, and I left after we had Isobel.

After witnessing the things I had seen in the police, I decided that I wanted to be at home with my family as much as I could, and thankfully James' job meant that this was possible for us. I will be forever grateful for that. While I wanted to be at home as much as I could, I still wanted to work as it was a huge part of my life. I retrained to become a teaching assistant.

Following my training, I applied for a job at a local school and was offered it. I initially worked one to one with two very incredible children, before becoming a general teaching assistant. I absolutely loved my job and truly believe that working with children, or being able to volunteer in a school, is just wonderful.

Whilst I was happy working part time, I felt that I wasn't really doing enough. I never felt like I was good enough. Being a mum had taken me over far more than I expected, and I realise now that I was possibly quite ill after having Jack. I felt somewhat isolated where I lived at the time, and I became completely obsessed with perfectionism. I worried so much that something would go wrong, and I was a huge stickler for a routine. I look back at some of the things I used to do and cringe now, but then I guess I did what I thought was best at the time, and isn't that all any of us can do?

Like so many people nowadays, I was always busy. Working, volunteering, taking the kids to places, socialising, exercising, sorting the house... it truly is never ending. For some reason, I never felt like I was doing enough. I had real issues with saying no, and I ended up taking on more and more. I was my own worst enemy as I would never ask for help and would usually refuse it when it was offered. I felt that if I couldn't do absolutely everything myself, I was a failure. It makes me sad to think about how I was back then...and it makes me sad knowing that so many people are living this life and will continue to live this way because they think that they have no other choice. I used to tell myself that only **I** could do certain things, because they needed to be done *'my way'*. It felt pointless asking other people to do things, because they wouldn't get it 'right' and so I may as well just do it all myself. I felt resentful a lot of the time, yet it was me doing it all to myself. Hindsight is a wonderful thing and I do believe that sometimes we need that big wakeup call before we will make the changes we need to, in order to make our lives better for ourselves.

I felt like I had to look after everyone else first, and that the more I took on, the better everyone else would be. I always put myself last. I told myself that it was ok though, and that it was even *supposed* to be like that! As a mum, surely I was meant to put everyone else first? As long as everyone else was happy, then that was what mattered.

Don't get me wrong here, I was not UNhappy... but I certainly wasn't as happy as I now realise I deserved to be (we **all** deserve to be happy, we just don't always see that as the truth). I was still being so unkind to myself.

I was pushing myself in every way. Mentally, physically, and emotionally. I was struggling with the idea of working part time as I somehow (ridiculously) felt like that made me inferior to anyone who worked full time. I put myself forward to do things I didn't always want to do, and I told myself that if I didn't offer, then nobody else would, and that would be a real shame.

In September 2018, without realising it, I was reaching my limit. I was working, volunteering, chair of the school PTA, taking the kids to activities five days of the week, organising social events, running up to 100 miles a month, keeping a pristine home, working an online make up business from my social media account... and worrying that I **still** wasn't doing enough.

I became unwell. 'Just a bit of a cold' I told myself. Ok, maybe a chest infection as it got worse. I dragged myself to work and said I was fine. My colleagues told me I probably shouldn't be in, and I assured them I would rest next week when it was half term (I still laugh at that... as IF anyone rests when they have kids at home). When it got to the point in class one day that I was struggling to breathe, my teacher insisted that I needed to see a doctor. I gave in, booked an appointment, and was told by the doctor that I had a severe chest infection and would need to take the rest of the week off, which I was *not* happy with. I was given a course of antibiotics, which didn't work; so then got a second course, which also didn't work. Steroids were next, although they put me in hospital for a night, and then some more tablets to try and sort it. The infection took a long time to clear. It left me exhausted. I thought having kids two years apart was exhausting... but this was a whole new level.

When the infection eventually cleared, I didn't pick up like I had expected to. I just couldn't shift the fatigue; I had never experienced anything like it. My whole body was so heavy. I felt like I was weighed down while wading through mud. It wasn't just my body either, my brain was struggling, and I couldn't think clearly at all.

I was back at the doctors every week for several weeks. After some time, I was told that I had Post Viral Fatigue and advised that it could last a few more weeks. I was horrified. I was a busy mum who needed to get back to work and all my other activities. I wanted to know what I could do to get myself better... something which didn't involve rest as I quite simply *didn't have time* to rest. I didn't have *time* to be ill. I felt like a malingerer and worried what people would be thinking about me, wondering why I wasn't getting better when I didn't appear to have anything wrong with me anymore.

I was mortified when my (luckily very good) doctor told me that the way things were going, I should be prepared that this could end up being M.E/CFS. I struggled to take it all in. There was no way this could be happening to me! I had always kept relatively fit and healthy... how could I become ill with something so serious? I didn't even really understand what M.E. was, so had no real idea of what was likely to happen to me. I knew that I had to do some research to find out more.

WHAT EVEN *IS* M.E?

M.E. stands for Myalgic Encephalomyelitis. Think it's hard to pronounce? (Mai-al-juhk-en-she-fuh-low-mai-uh-lai-tuhs) Try getting your head around what it actually is! It can also be referred to as Chronic Fatigue Syndrome (CFS)... which unfortunately leads some people to believe that it's all about being 'tired'.

It is one seriously frustrating illness, for so many reasons. Starting with the fact that experts still don't know what causes it. While there are several theories, and there seems to be common starting points for a lot of people who have it, there's no definitive cause. It has been suggested that causes could be viral infections, bacterial infections, problems with the immune system, a hormone imbalance, stress, emotional issues or even your genes.

There are currently no specific tests for diagnosing M.E. which makes it much harder to identify... and sometimes much harder to be believed when you do get ill. It is usually diagnosed based on an individual's symptoms and by ruling out other conditions which could be causing them. To be diagnosed, you must have a series of tests to rule out other illnesses. This can obviously take a long time, and it's not uncommon for an official diagnosis to take up to a couple of years, or even longer, which is so discouraging, not to mention scary.

Symptoms can vary massively between individuals. There are different levels of severity, with some people struggling with manageable symptoms which affect day to day life in a small (but still very significant) way, to some people being so severely affected that they end up being bed bound, unable to look after themselves in any way.

The most common symptoms include chronic fatigue; being unable to feel rested even after sleep; taking a long time to recover after any physical (or even mental) activities; problems sleeping and problems with memory, concentration and thinking. There can be a whole range of other symptoms too, including muscle/joint pain, headaches, sore throat, feeling dizzy, feeling nauseous, flu-like symptoms and heart palpitations. Symptoms can vary from day to day, or even hour to hour. You literally never know how you will wake up feeling, or how you may feel within the next hour. Planning to do anything is hard, as sometimes there is no warning that things will change for the worse.

Obviously, feeling like this takes its toll on you and so it is very common for people with M.E. to have additional emotional problems too. Anxiety, panic attacks and even depression can follow on from being so ill and can make things so much worse. A lot of people may believe that people with M.E. have depression rather than M.E. and it can be hard to explain to people what is going on.

Unfortunately, at the time of writing this, there is no cure for M.E. and no official medical treatment which is proven to help everyone. It is very much trial and error, and there have been huge mistakes made in trying to help people with M.E. People have been guided to do things which have ended up making them a lot worse. Research into M.E. is massively underfunded and awareness of it is quite low too, which means that people who get diagnosed with it often do not receive the support they desperately need. Doctors often prescribe medication to try to control symptoms such as pain and sleeping problems, but obviously this can have a big impact when those symptoms are not going away or getting better over time. There is guidance on how to learn to live with M.E. and manage it, including things like Cognitive Behavioural Therapy (CBT), but these can only help people live with it, rather than cure it.

Advice can be given in how to make appropriate lifestyle changes, including diet, resting, exercise, energy management, relaxing and supplements. As people with M.E. have such different experiences with it, it can be difficult to find anything which will help absolutely everyone.

It is currently estimated that approximately 250, 000 people in the UK are affected by M.E. and around 17 million people worldwide may have it (Action For ME 2022). While M.E. is listed as a specific medical condition in the 2010 Equality Act, this does not mean that everyone with a diagnosis is automatically classed as having a disability. This can lead to lots of problems for people who are unable to work due to how ill they are when they try to claim benefits.

There is not enough medical evidence to show that complimentary therapy can help symptoms of M.E. and most of these therapies are not available on the NHS, unless you have a very good doctor who is willing to recommend that you need them. Diet changes and paying for additional supplements can end up being expensive... meaning that M.E. can have huge financial implications too, which will cause even more of a burden for sufferers.

The way a lot of people think now is that doctors can always find answers for us and will help to sort us out. It is therefore very frustrating when they can't. (I imagine it must be also frustrating for the doctors themselves.)

I personally advocate a truly holistic approach to dealing with M.E. I think it is important to be open to *anything* and *everything* which may help. I had to accept that some things may or may not help, and even that some things would help at one point, but not another. I think both complimentary treatments **and** modern medicine have a place in managing this illness, and everything should be available to M.E. sufferers. While I do believe that anyone **can** get better and that mindset is **the** biggest thing which will help anyone to recover, there can be no denying that there are certain things which can help, and everyone should be able to have access to them, in the same way that patients of other illnesses are prescribed treatments.

It is so important that as much awareness as possible is raised about this terrible, debilitating and life changing illness. People need to be aware that it is not just 'being tired', and much more help needs to be made available. Support is also important for carers of people with M.E. as I know from my own experience how much my loved ones were affected. That does not help with the feelings of guilt you have when you are ill and can hinder recovery.

My hope is that one day, M.E. will have the same support as other serious illnesses, and it will be easily treatable.

It is also worth mentioning at this point, that Long Covid has many similarities to M.E., and I truly believe that everything within this book could help people who have this. So many people have had Covid, and it is very strange how it has affected people so differently. In many ways it can be very similar to M.E. in that there does not always appear to be an explanation as to why one person will experience very mild symptoms and go on to make a full recovery, while someone else can end up becoming seriously unwell, and then having ongoing symptoms. At the time of writing this book, Covid is still doing the rounds, and I believe that it is highly likely that even if/when it disappears, something else could arise to take its place. I feel that people dealing with Long Covid need to look at their lives overall, in the way that I was forced to through having M.E. and decide to commit to themselves to have the best chance of recovery possible.

ME WITH M.E.

When my GP first told me that she thought I may end up being diagnosed with M.E. I struggled to take it in. Although I didn't really know that much about it, I knew enough to know that it was serious and that there was no cure. A friend had recently been diagnosed with it and I knew that his life had changed from being a very full on, active one, to a vastly different one which saw him in a world of pain and exhaustion, with no end in sight. I could not believe that my life was possibly going to go that way.

My GP was very empathetic and luckily warned me about something very early on which I found quite hard to accept at first. She warned me that lots of people would not take my illness seriously, or even believe that I was ill. She said that unfortunately, people in the medical profession would be included in that group of disbelieving people. I was astonished at this because I was so, so ill...how could it not be taken seriously? She confessed that she had previously been a doctor who had difficulty believing in M.E. and such illnesses herself, until her own partner had started suffering. She had seen first-hand the drastic changes in his life and so could no longer dispute that it was a 'real' illness, and one which was **not** in the mind, as many people will suggest. She warned me that people would say uneducated, and sometimes even potentially hurtful things, as they did not know much about it.

Going home that day, I struggled to get across to James what she had said. Partly because I simply couldn't remember a lot of it at the time. I guess part of it was shock, but at that time, the dreaded 'brain fog' was starting to make more of an impact.

When I first became unwell with a chest infection, it had hit me hard. Looking back, I can see that my body had been trying to send me signals to slow down and look after myself properly for a long time; but I had been ignoring it. I was too ***busy*** to slow down. I had *so* much to do all the time. People relied on me, so how could I stop doing the things I was doing? Plus, I always felt guilty for taking any time off or time out for **me**. Even my exercise was done at times which meant that I could either co-ordinate it with socialising, or else I would go before anyone else in the house was up, simply so that I was not taking myself away from anyone who would need me in any way.

When I got ill, I still didn't stop. I pushed myself into work and carried on doing all the other things I was doing. I told myself that it was *just* a cold, then *just* a chest infection. I compared myself with other people who would also push through illness and so kept on going. Then when I was told by the doctor that I could not go to work, I felt horribly guilty, even though everyone at school was glad that I was not coming in, as they had all been telling me to stay away. I still put myself under pressure. Totally unnecessary pressure-but that's just how I was.

I kept waiting to feel better and I just couldn't understand why I wasn't doing. I couldn't get my head around why I was starting to feel worse. It made no sense. I told myself I was resting properly (I actually wasn't). I was eating quite healthily (or so I thought). I had stopped exercising, so my body was more rested. Why wasn't I improving?

Gradually, more symptoms crept up on me. I had been getting worried about the different symptoms. Once I had been told about post viral fatigue, I had (as I think a lot of us do nowadays) turned to good old 'Dr Google' and had come up with a whole range of possibilities of what I may have. I was scared.

The doctor explained to me that I would need a series of tests, as the diagnosis of M.E. generally comes from eliminating a range of other illnesses. She warned me that this would take some time and that a professional diagnosis could even take up to a couple of years, depending on how fast I could get everything done. You usually need to have had symptoms for a minimum of six months before a doctor will officially class it as M.E. I couldn't believe that it could take so long.

My doctor got me set up with all the various tests I needed. I saw several specialists and had **lots** of blood tests. My blood tests initially showed up a couple of things which needed further investigation, and while I was worried, I did hope that they would show up something which could be cured, as the thought of having something incurable was incomprehensible.

I saw an ENT specialist, a Rheumatologist, had an MRI scan and CAT scans.... and other things along the way, some of which I simply can't remember now as my memory was not great in any way! I had blood tests galore and felt like I was always at my doctors. I hated being there as I felt bad for taking up her time, although thankfully she never made me feel like that. It was so annoying that nothing was being found which could be easily sorted. My bloods were fine, all my levels were pretty much normal, and nothing really needed tweaking. People were asking me whether I needed more iron, more vitamin D, more vitamin B... but I was at, or even above, the recommended level for all of these. I had a couple of comments about whether I was 'just depressed' which galled me in so many ways! Firstly, that anyone could use the word 'just' in front of anything to do with depression given how serious depression is... and secondly, that I knew that people thought that the illness was all in my head, which I knew it wasn't.

My symptoms were getting progressively worse. What had started with fatigue and being unable to pick myself up after my infection, was gradually becoming a living hell.

I felt like I had flu permanently. I ached all over, my head pounded, my throat was constantly sore, and I felt sick a lot of the time. I would get dizzy quite often, which had a big effect on me. My body temperature was all over the place, going from sweating one minute to being freezing cold the next. My feet and hands sometimes went white they were so cold. Brain fog would hit, where I had anywhere from either mild, or quite severe concentration and memory problems. Embarrassingly, my speech would go slurred, and I sounded like I was drunk. I was just so exhausted at times that I simply couldn't get my words out and everything became such an effort.

The fatigue was horrific. I had thought I knew what exhaustion was after having a job where you could sometimes be working for 18 hours non-stop, and I certainly felt exhausted when I had my children... but this was a whole new level. You couldn't explain it and it was horrible when people would say flippant things like "Oh I must have this M.E. too, because I'm always tired". It was heart-breaking thinking that people believed that they knew what I felt like, because they got tired a lot. There is absolutely NO comparison between the level of exhaustion you get through anything else with serious illnesses such as M.E.

With the fatigue came pain. All over body pain. Some days were just so much to cope with that I wasn't sure how I was getting through. Writing about this now and revisiting that pain in my mind has made me cry as I can't believe the level of pain I felt daily and the emotions which were attached to it.

My doctor was prescribing me pain killers and tablets to help me sleep, as sleep was such a struggle. It seems crazy that when you are so exhausted you can't always sleep... but pain has an efficient way of keeping you awake.

I absolutely hated taking all the tablets I was being prescribed. After having spent a decade in the police, I was all too aware of how easy it is to become addicted to painkillers and other medication, and I was really frightened that it could happen to me. The painkillers would work for a short time, but then wouldn't touch the pain after a while, so I would need something else. Inevitably, I always needed higher doses or stronger painkillers. Then I would need tablets to counterbalance some of the effects of some of the strong painkillers. The tablets which helped me sleep did help with the sleep, but the side effects were awful. They made me feel even more like a zombie than I already did. I felt like I was in a no-win situation, and it was difficult to see a way out.

After going through many tests over a six-month period, I was then referred to an M.E. specialist in Manchester. My mother-in-law kindly took me to my appointments as there was no way I could drive that far. She also came into the appointments too, which was a Godsend as I simply couldn't articulate everything I had to say sometimes, and I couldn't remember everything I was being told.

The M.E. doctor was fantastic, and it was great to see someone who specialised in what I was going through. I had to go through a whole load of blood tests again so that she could be sure that there was nothing which had been missed. When she gave me the official diagnosis, it felt strange.

I was partly glad that I had a name to what I was going through and felt reassured that it wasn't all 'in my head'. I hadn't suddenly become 'lazy', and I wasn't alone. It was also hard to accept, as it meant that I was officially more ill than I would have liked to ever admit to. I sometimes felt like the diagnosis meant more to other people, as now they could see that I had an 'official' illness with a 'proper' name.

Unfortunately, the diagnosis did not mean that I suddenly had hope – as I was all too aware that I now had an illness with no medical cure and no official treatment; as well as knowing that I would not even be believed by some people as to the seriousness of it.

I was referred through to the NHS Chronic Fatigue Services and while they helped in giving advice and some coping tools, I was also advised that I should not expect to ever get fully better. While I appreciate that false hope may not be a good thing, I found this to be really disheartening, especially as I was so determined to get better.

I told myself that I would do whatever it took to get better. However, the truth of it was that at times, giving energy to something which felt hopeless was quite often too much to do. I **wanted** to get better more than anything, but I just didn't have the energy to do the things I sometimes needed to. I got stuck in a cycle of misery. I felt so scared and worried... and sorry for myself! I wondered what I had done to deserve this. I looked at other people who had been just as busy as I had been and wondered what they had done differently to make them get through illnesses. I mentally beat myself up so much, telling myself that I must be weak; I must be a failure.

At the time of me becoming unwell, I was working part time as a teaching assistant in a local school. My own children were at this school, and I absolutely hated feeling like I was letting everyone down by not being there. I had tried to go back a couple of times, and it was so painful, in so many ways. I was physically exhausted, couldn't concentrate and it was mentally draining... even just listening to a few children read was beyond me. When my friend asked me if I wanted to have a brew in the staff room, I sadly replied that I couldn't as there was no way I could manage to walk up the stairs. I had to accept that there was no way I could carry on working. I had to make a choice... to have hopefully enough energy to look after my own children or to give my energy to doing my job and looking after other people's children. While there is obviously no real choice when you put it like that, it was still a heart-breaking and difficult decision.

As well as having to give up my job, I had to give up volunteering. I was enjoying helping with Rainbows and Beavers as my children were at them at the time. Obviously, that became too much for me. I also had to quit exercising. I have always kept fit and so I hated having to give this up. While I was in the police, I was a real gym bunny, going three to four times a week for a few hours at a time, as well as regularly running. After having my children, I stuck with running and loved it. Pre-illness I was running up to 100 miles a month. There was no way I could even think about running any more though. Some days, I couldn't even get out of bed myself!

Socialising went out of the window. I had a great social life before M.E. I enjoyed going out with my friends, with my family and with my husband. I was the 'organiser' and rarely a weekend went by where we didn't have plans. We kept very busy and had a very active social life.

It wasn't just the big things which I lost though; it was the things that we often take for granted. It was being able to drive. It was being able to walk some days. It was being able to get myself to the bathroom. It was being able to shower without having to lie down for an hour after.

Some days I could cook a meal for us all... and others I would need assistance simply with eating my food. Some days I could go and pick the kids up and others I couldn't even get myself dressed. At times I could go for a short family walk... yet sometimes I couldn't even pick up a book without it physically hurting.

I found that each day was different and there was no real way of telling what each day would be like. Sometimes it would even change hour by hour and take me massively by surprise. I learnt that if I exerted myself in any way, I would pay for it with a lot of extra pain and exhaustion. This made it difficult as I wanted to be able to do things, and so would battle to do something, whilst always anticipating that the payback for it would be horrific.

I worked so hard to put a brave face on. I didn't want people realising **just** how bad I was, as I felt so pathetic. Even though I had done a lot of research on M.E. I still struggled with the concept of it. I couldn't quite get my head around the fact that there was no real explanation as to why **my** body was doing this... or that there was no actual cure for it. I kept hoping that one day I would wake up and feel better. I hoped that there would be some sort of medical breakthrough and I would suddenly be presented with some sort of treatment which would help.

Life continued, as it always does. I kept on keeping on in my new way. Things got worse. I had less and less energy, and more and more pain. I couldn't remember what it felt like to not feel like this. My fatigue was horrific. My body and throat were constantly sore. Brain fog, slurred speech, dizziness, falling over... all these symptoms were now just part of everyday life.

Some days were much better than others. These were the most dangerous days as these were the days that I wanted to believe that maybe I was getting better. These were also the days where I would push myself. I would tell myself that I may as well get the most out of feeling ok and do the things I wanted to. The days where I would try and pretend to my children that mummy was fine, and we could do things which I couldn't do on my 'bad' days. These days only made me even more ill.

I would push myself and the payback would be horrendous. It was so, so hard. I desperately wanted my old life back. I wanted to be pain and symptom free. I wanted to work again, to exercise, to volunteer, to be sociable. Hell, I wanted to be able to go to the bloody toilet on my own or to not worry that halfway through a meal I would become so tired that I would have to put my head on the table and wait for my husband to help me upstairs to bed. I wanted out of this nightmare... but it seemed that there was no real way out.

I had done lots of research, some of which went in, although a lot of it didn't. I was trying lots of different things. I would give them a bit of time, but then when I didn't see the improvements I was hoping for, I would class them as being hopeless and give up. I was not living the best life I could with my illness, as I was mentally punishing myself, and I was failing to do the things which would *truly* help me.

I was spending a fortune in trying different things, but again without giving all of them a fair chance. I was so desperate for a 'quick fix'.

One of the things I really hated was when my mobility became a struggle. I had to buy myself a walking stick. This certainly is a way of making an invisible illness suddenly become more visible. I would get stared at by people I didn't know and get a pitying look from some of the people I did know. While my kids eventually got used to seeing me with it, they really hated that I had to have it to. People would ask me whether I had been involved in an accident and I hated having to reply with what was wrong with me, because invariably I would get the same things said to me "Oh, you don't look ill", "Is that where you get tired?" "Is that the same as yuppy flu?" "I had a friend with that, she got better though meditating, have you tried that?"

After a while I learned to have a different relationship with my stick, in that I looked at it as a way of giving me extra freedom and time spent with my family, but it was truly hard. I hated when someone 40 years older than me would whizz past me and stop to throw me a sympathetic look. But needs must... and I needed my stick. So, I swallowed my pride, treated myself to a snazzy stick after a while, and learned to walk with my head held high (even if that only happened for a short time as my head got very heavy when I was out and about).

The Covid pandemic hit when I was ill. Boy did that take its toll on me. In some ways, I felt that I had already become isolated due to being unable to leave the house very often and not seeing people the way I had done, so that part of lockdown wasn't as bad for me personally as it could have been. I was not prepared however, for us all being at home all the time, or the intensity of home school!! My energy now had to go into being available for my children**... all** the time. As ill as I was, I still took my job as home-school teacher seriously and it truly exhausted me. Plus, it massively stressed me out, which made my symptoms worse.

Unfortunately, one thing which will always live with me from this, is the fact that my children believed that I was dying. They were at home with me 24/7 during the Covid lockdowns and so my brave face couldn't be on all the time. They saw how I was so ill that sometimes I couldn't get out of bed. They saw me struggling to walk, to talk, to eat or to dress myself. We played a game of 'Who can help get mummy's socks on the fastest' when they saw me struggling to even do that, which is not really the kind of games you would wish to ever play! I had always been a very active mum. I was the mum who got involved with everything, took them everywhere, had their friends over, played games and raced with them, organised so many fun things and barely kept still. I was the energetic mum who forced herself to keep going even when I didn't really feel up to it - because I thought that is what a 'good mum' should do.

The difference when I became unwell was huge. From being that energetic mum, to being a mum who sometimes cried because her children's voices were too loud and cringed from hugs because they hurt her body. I couldn't watch TV with them because the TV hurt my eyes. I had to say no...all the time. Writing this is difficult because I have worked so hard to overcome emotions like guilt, but I feel it rear its ugly head when I focus on this part! (I **do** know that being ill will never make anyone a bad parent and with all the work I have done on myself, I can thankfully now overcome that guilt.)

During lockdown, we had an incident when we were doing some painting together as a family, and our son Jack got really upset. After chatting for a while, he finally confessed that he was really worried about me. He thought I was dying. He said that he couldn't believe that I was so ill and not dying. He thought that we must be keeping a secret from him, as there was no way he could accept that I wasn't getting any better and so assumed I must be dying. That was so heart-breaking. He had been trying to put on this brave face, while inside he was worrying all the time. Our daughter later told us that she worried about it too. I already knew that James had been extra worried when Covid hit, as he had told me that he didn't believe that I was strong enough to survive it if I got it.

This is the part which other people don't always realise when one person gets ill. It is never just **one** person who is affected by illness: it's a whole set of family members and friends. It is truly awful. While I never want to take away from the pain of the person dealing with the illness itself, I do think it is so important that people who are helping that person are recognised for their own struggles too.

Our lives had changed so much. Things we used to take for granted as a family had to change. If I felt well enough to do something fun, I would suffer in my body, and my family would suffer watching me in pain. Days out switched to days in. Late nights as a treat at the weekend became mummy going to bed earlier than the kids. Household chores which, thankfully, the kids had always helped with from being little (as I'm a big believer in everyone helping when your part of a team) became such that the kids **had** to do things now because I no longer could. While it was great that they were learning life skills which I know will help them in the future, this is not the way I would have chosen for them to learn them.

We carried on as best we could. While I may be painting a bleak picture here, you can be sure of one thing, we were still blessed with love, and for that I will be forever grateful.

Then one week, everything changed. I decided to clean a bit more than I normally would one day when the kids were back at school. I knew that while I was doing it, it was a bad idea. But I had a little bit more energy, and I told myself that now the kids were back I would probably be ok. How wrong I was.

That half hour of cleaning put me in bed. For a week. It got to the point where James was having to help me out of bed practically every time I needed to get out. I needed his help to go to the bathroom. I couldn't leave the house, never mind pick the kids up. I couldn't make tea and was struggling with the effort of even eating. I kept quiet, as my voice was slurring so badly. I needed my walking stick around the house (which was a real low as that truly brought it home to the kids how bad I was). I couldn't watch TV, or read, or pick up my phone without it all hurting too much. The light was painful, so I needed the curtains shut. I was constantly cold. My symptoms were in massive flare up and I couldn't sleep, even though I was beyond exhausted.

I was scared. We were all scared. James and I talked about the fact that if this continued, I was going to have to accept that I needed to consider getting a wheelchair. I had needed to use one a few times previously and I hated it, so I was devastated at the thought that this was now becoming a real possibility. It had taken me so long to accept that I needed a walking stick, but this was a world apart from that.

As awful as it sounds (and it truly was), that week was possibly the best thing that could have happened to me.

That week was the week that I genuinely changed my mindset. Forever. It was the week that I fully accepted that my recovery was all down to **me**. There was no point waiting for a quick fix. No hoping for a miracle cure. No waiting for more research to be done so that more treatments may become available. No more trying something for a couple of weeks and then giving up. This was all on me.

James had told me on several occasions that I needed to treat my recovery as a full-time job. Whilst I knew this was probably true, I couldn't accept it. I wasn't ready to do that... because it felt selfish. My personality traits meant that I wanted to put others first. I didn't want to put myself first, even if it meant that I was becoming more and more ill. Although I was a big advocate of 'self-care isn't selfish', I wasn't truly walking the walk, because I personally felt selfish. I was great at giving advice, and I would happily give up my precious energy to help anyone and everyone else... but I still wasn't treating myself with the love and respect that I deserved and needed.

That week of being fully bed bound changed my ideas on all of that. I knew that actually, I **was** being selfish in not putting myself first. I realised that if I didn't focus fully on my recovery, then I would simply become more and more ill. And to me, that made me feel like I would become more of a failure. When I looked five years into the future, I realised that I wanted to have a life which didn't involve bed days (unless it was through choice), walking sticks or wheelchairs. I wanted to be walking, running, and playing with my kids. I wanted to get rid of the fear which preyed on me whenever I did anything fun. I wanted to recover as best as I could and that was down to **me**. Nobody else could do it for me. I had to accept help of course (nobody can do anything alone without help) ... but I needed to put into action the things I needed to do to get myself better.

I decided to make a commitment... to myself.

I worked out in my head what I planned to do, then sat with James and went through it all. He was absolutely delighted and promised to fully support me. We spoke to the kids too and told them what was going on so they would know what to expect. As a family, I knew I wanted us all to be on the same page because support is one of the most important things when you have something like this to cope with.

I decided that I would fully commit to my new plan for a minimum of six months. I knew any less would not be giving it a fair chance. I did say that even if things hadn't improved in six months though, I would keep going as I really believed in all of the changes I was planning to make, but six months seemed like a reasonable time to be able to assess where I was up to.

Six months may seem like a long time... but they are going to (hopefully) pass in everyone's life anyway! I would rather have six months of trying my best at something, rather than six months of continuing with the way things were and getting progressively worse, which I knew was the other option.

I was **ready** to recover. That may seem like a strange thing to say, because you would assume that anybody who is unwell would be ready to get better. But (and this may not be the nicest thing to hear...but I promise that I say it with love, and with the knowledge that this was me personally), I was not ready to get better as I was not willing to do *anything* and *everything* it took to get myself better. I was making excuses. I did not want to give up certain things because I felt like I had already had so much taken away from me that I didn't want something else removed from my life. I didn't want to feel selfish in giving up time I could do other things to time spent purely on me. I didn't want to say no to certain things and people. I still wanted the 'quick fix' or some sort of magic pill. I didn't want to put the hard work in to myself. I felt exhausted just thinking about, never mind doing, some of the things I knew I needed to do. I had got stuck in my own pity party if the truth be known. I was the victim in my own story and the world outside had started to become a bit scarier. That may sound pathetic, but I can guarantee I will not be the only person who has felt or currently feels like that.

I decided that only **I** had the power to change the ending of my own story. I committed to myself... and got to work.

What follows is everything I have done to aid my recovery. I truly believe that anybody who gets ill has their own journey to go on and what will work for one person may not work for another. It truly is about trial and error, especially with an illness such as M.E. One of the most important things you must do in my opinion, is to be willing to find your **true** self through this illness and subsequent recovery.

Nothing that I have done over my recovery period which I am choosing to write about in this book should be harmful in any way. All the things I suggest in here, you will have likely heard before. I'm not going to give you a new spin on anything, simply, I will give you *my* spin on it. I'm no medical expert, I'm no scientist, I won't confuse you with expert guidance, because a lot of the expert guidance bamboozles me! What I write is simple and easy to understand (although I appreciate that if you are struggling with M.E., it may take a long time to read and use up a lot of energy, so I pray that it really **is** worth it for you). While my primary hope is that this book will help people with M.E. fibromyalgia and Long Covid, I also truly hope that it can help people who *don't* have M.E too, as it is all about things which could help anyone, no matter what they may be going through with life. Being willing to work on yourself, and then putting that work in, is by far the **best** thing you can ever do. For yourself, and also for everyone around you.

PART 2

MY RECOVERY ACTIONS

This part of the book will cover all the things which I focused on when I decided to commit to my recovery. I have separated them into sections so that it is easier to read and different things can be focused on individually as needed.

MINDSET

When people ask me what the most important thing I have done in my recovery, I have absolutely no doubt that it has been working on my mindset.

I truly believe that once you get your mindset right, you can deal with anything and everything. I won't say that things become *easy*, because things can still be difficult, but they get easier when you are in the right frame of mind.

While I don't believe I have ever had a 'bad' mindset, I used to be a bit of a pessimist on the sly. It will probably surprise people who didn't know me very well, as I always appeared to be a positive and happy-go-lucky person. But inside, I was always worrying. I would have classed myself as a natural born worrier. I also told myself that being so concerned was 'in my genes', and so assumed that there wouldn't be much I could do about it.

I would often look towards the worst-case scenario. I would plan for things while working out what I would need to do if the worst was to happen. I told myself that this simply meant I would always be prepared. In reality, I was adding to my own stress by focusing on things which may never even happen, which is such a waste of time and precious energy.

When I had my son Jack, my fear went into overdrive. We had sadly lost a baby before we had him, and I think that really affected me as a mum. I worried all through my pregnancy and I kept expecting something bad to happen. When we had him, I got myself into such a strict routine which I told myself was keeping him safe. I convinced myself that if I didn't stick rigidly to this routine, something would go wrong. We unfortunately lost another baby before then going on to have our daughter Isobel, so that further added to my anxieties over having children. I had hoped I would be more carefree with a second child... but if anything, I was probably worse!

I didn't believe I was a 'negative' person though, and still tried my best to see the good in things... but I wouldn't say it came naturally to me in the past.

A couple of years before I got ill, my husband had joined a group via his work which focused on personal and professional development. With it came a lot of motivational speakers, book recommendations and what I would refer to as 'self-help'. I remember him trying to talk to me about some of the things he was learning about... and I was quite simply not very interested! I didn't think that I needed any help, thought I was positive enough and didn't really see how reading a book or listening to a podcast would genuinely help me. I was just getting through life as best I could and didn't think I needed to work on my mindsight. How naïve I was!

I did get into 'self-help' when I started an online business. It was highly recommended and although I resisted at first, I eventually decided to see what it was all about. I soon realised that I absolutely loved it! I was listening to and reading things which really resonated with me and helped me feel better about certain things which had gone on in my life. I couldn't believe that I hadn't been involved in this earlier. James would laugh as I would enthusiastically tell him about a book I was reading or listening to which I thought he would love... and he would tell me that he had tried recommending it to me a few months ago!

I jumped on the 'self-help bandwagon' and began filling my mind with good stuff... but if I'm honest, I wasn't always doing the things which I was happy to promote. I would spout off positive quotes and fill my social media feed with positivity, but I wasn't always following the things I would say to others. I was still all about making other people feel better and putting their needs before my own. I whole-heartedly believed in everything I was saying, but I just couldn't always get it right myself. I would tell people that they should be kind to themselves, and that self-care wasn't selfish... I was still verbally beating myself up and experiencing a lot of self-criticism. I was working so hard on looking after everyone else and was not putting myself first, as, to me, that felt selfish. I told myself that I was happy if everyone else was happy. There were a lot of people to try and make happy though, and so it was easy to get caught up in that and find myself sometimes unhappy... but feeling it was ok because at least others around me felt happy. It's not really a healthy way of living... and yet it's one which so many of us do.

When I got ill, it was so unexpected. I thought that I was doing well. I was eating what I thought was a healthy diet, I was exercising, working in a job I loved, volunteering, I had a happy marriage, a wonderful family, a good group of friends and a great social life. I was living life to the full and enjoying it. So, when I took a first look at my life, I couldn't work out what I could be possibly doing 'wrong'. I don't think I was necessarily doing anything 'wrong' even now - so if you are reading this and thinking that you do all of the above, please don't think that I am suggesting that **you** are doing or have done anything wrong, (or even that you may get ill if you aren't unwell now). I do think that it's always worth taking the time out to sit and really evaluate your life and look at whether there is enough real time for **you** yourself doing the things you truly love, without it being something which is more for everyone else. One thing I wasn't really doing, was doing anything which was purely for **me**.

Anything that I was doing for me always had a little caveat attached to it. Even exercise, which you could argue was for me as it kept me fit and healthy, had a condition with it. I would exercise at times where it didn't interfere with anyone else. I would get up before anyone in the house was up, so I was still fully available for my family. Or I would run in the evenings when the kids were in bed so that I had helped with the bedtime routine; even though my husband had absolutely no issue with me running before they went to bed... it was **me** putting the pressure on me.

When I look now, I will comment that for me personally, the illness M.E. has the clue in its initials... I needed **me** time. Of course, I had not expected, and certainly did not want it in the way I got it. I definitely would not wish it on anyone else, as it is truly horrific. One of the reasons I decided to write this book is in the hope that if even one person reads it and looks at their own life and makes some helpful changes, then it will all have been worth it. Whether you as a reader have M.E. or not, I really believe that we should all have that me time... and it should come (and this is often the tricky part) **guilt free**.

Oh guilt... how often it has plagued my days! Guilt is the most ridiculous emotion, although it does serve a genuine purpose. It is there to help us realise that we have done something wrong, for us to learn lessons and make sure we don't do that again. It has however become totally abused and a way of life for so many of us.

When I had my children, I experienced an awful amount of mum guilt. I felt guilty for doing anything for me, like I was somehow taking away from my kids. I felt like everything should be about them, and even though I still did things with other people, and for myself, I would feel so guilty at times that it took a lot of my enjoyment away. It was awful. Things have been made worse by the fact that it has kind of become normal for parents to openly berate themselves either in real life or on social media. It's now seemingly ok to call yourself a 'bad mum', or 'worst dad ever', because you have done something like (horror of horrors) forgotten it was non uniform day, turned up late for a party, been unable to attend a meeting because you had to work, not been able to afford to buy something, or shouted at your children in public for doing something wrong. There are people abusing their own children out there... but woe betide me if the tooth fairy didn't deliver... # WORST MUM EVER!!!!!! (For the record, I absolutely detest this hashtag and think it, and other similar ones berating ourselves, should be banned.)

It is so silly, and completely unnecessary. Yet it really has become something I see so much of. Rather than applauding ourselves for doing what is essentially the hardest, most underpaid, undervalued job ever, for which you have no instructions... we criticise ourselves! It's so sad.

Guilt isn't only for parents though. It extends to being a daughter/son, or sibling. You can be a bad friend, or a terrible employer/employee. Add on top of that feelings of guilt for the things we eat, (or don't eat) the exercise we do (or don't do), the housework we do (or don't do), the money we spend on things (or don't spend), the time we have off if we get sick, the time we spend watching TV, the people we feel we let down... there is a never ending supply of things we can make ourselves feel guilty about. It has such a detrimental effect on our wellbeing.

Throw into the equation the comparison game, and things get even harder. How many of us are guilty of comparing our lives, or aspects of it, to other peoples? Again, whether in real life, or via social media... it seems much more common now for us to do this. Social media especially has made it so much easier for us all to be able to compare ourselves with what our friends, family, colleagues, and often even complete strangers are doing! What we tend to forget, is that social media usually only show people's highlights, rather than the bad bits! I say that social media is like a photo album you are making. You would choose the best pictures to show, rather than the ones where you are blinking, or your child has his/her finger up their nose, or it's all blurred! You pick the best pictures and put them in a photo album, or up on display in the house, so that you can remember things fondly. Social media is pretty much the same...except it's ongoing. Every day you can choose to portray your highlights. Even if you don't post every day, when you do post, you tend to choose the best things to show. The holidays, the promotions, the engagements, the weddings, the new babies, the weight loss, the new job, the kids good school reports, the awards achieved, the days out, the nights out.... all the good bits! Even if the day has been a bit of a let-down, we can still choose to find the best pictures and rave about what a wonderful day it has been, what wonderful friends we have and how lucky we are!

I think social media has a lot of effect on people's mindset now, both good and bad. I love that there are so many groups and people who take time with spreading positivity... but it can be all too easy to fall into the 'scroll hole' and find that you have spent hours of your day aimlessly looking through other people's lives and making yourself feel worse about your own.

Tackling your mindset may be one of, if not THE biggest challenges, you may face in life, especially if you are ill. When I decided to fully focus on getting my mindset in a good place, I quickly realised that this would be a lifetime commitment. I accepted that there would always be times where I would struggle, as well as times where things would be easier. I knew that I would have to ask for, and accept, help along the way. This has never been a strength of mine if I'm honest. I had always prided myself on being the person who people came to for help. The person who people knew they could rely on. The person who would never say no... even if not saying no made me miserable, or even ill. I struggled with the concept of saying no, as I felt that I was letting people down. What I had to learn was that by saying yes to everything, meant that I was saying no to myself and my own health and wellbeing. That's not a good recipe for having a good mindset... or a healthy life. There is only ever so much any one person can take on. It's hard when you look at people who appear to have it all together. But the truth of it is, the people who genuinely **do** have it all together (most of the time anyway) are the people who ask for, and accept, help.

People aren't meant to be alone, we should all accept help from others. We have all got relationships with others and should use them to help us survive, and even better, to thrive. Relationships can be with family, friends, colleagues, neighbours, professionals, people we meet in the street or people who serve us in a shop! One thing which would really help us, was if we all felt able to ask for help, and to accept help. It has taken me a long time to get to this point in my life, and I can guarantee that there will be people reading this thinking 'There's no way I can do that because it's **me** who is the helper!' and I get it... I really, really do! When I was ill at the start, I really struggled to ask for, or to accept help. Even when people were asking what they could do for me, I would say "Oh nothing, thank you." **Even** when people were offering help which would have ultimately helped James and the kids, I would say no, because I didn't want to put anyone else out! I was so conditioned to think that asking for help was selfish and weak. I worried that it would put pressure on other people.

Now, there is a fine line here. Because while it's important that we do accept help, it's hard knowing that the people who tend to offer help are often the ones (like me) who may be struggling and overwhelmed themselves. That can be a big factor to accepting help I know. We don't want to burden people who we know have a lot on their own plates! But what you must remember is that you don't have to ask for help every single day of your life from the same person. So, if someone is offering their help/support, then *please* do accept it.

The other tough thing with regards to help, is always offering it when you are exhausted yourself. Again, it's hard learning to say no, but you **must** prioritise yourself as much as you can. Of course, there will always be times where you do need to help others, no matter what. But if you are in a situation yourself where you are really struggling, it's absolutely fine to explain to someone that you may not be in a position right *now* to offer the help you normally could, but you will happily do it when things are a bit easier for you.

Mindset is a big buzzword now. We hear about it all the time, but I guess when I looked at it, I didn't really know how to improve mine. Of course, I was making lots of changes and I knew they would all help, but I realised that it was mindset which would be the ultimate thing I needed to sort. There was no good changing my diet, if my mindset meant that I would slip back into old ways when I didn't feel 100%. It was no good telling myself I would get outside every day, when my mindset was such that when bad weather hit, I would tell myself it was ok to give it a miss. I needed to be fully committed to myself... and having the strongest mindset was the way I knew I would do my best.

There are thousands of books and guides out there which can help you have a positive mindset... but no amount of reading or guidance can truly make you have one unless you are committed to having one. Life is hard, and there are times where all we want to do is crawl into bed and not come out again. Even when things are going well, so many of us may be waiting for something bad to happen. It's like we have been conditioned to believe that good things never last. We tell ourselves (and others) that it's all going too well, or that something is bound to burst our bubble, or that bad things come in threes when one bad thing happens. We seem to be ok with focusing on the negatives in our lives and we can thrive on misery. That might sound strange, and you may not want to believe it... but all you have to do is watch the news, or a soap or drama, or even get chatting to somebody and you will often find that the focus on negativity is pretty strong.

People who seem upbeat and naturally positive can even feel ridiculed at times for being this way. Sometimes people seem to get irritated by people who always seem happy and may even call them out, making out that they are fake.

Surely we should all want to be positive? I'm not talking about grinning and baring it for the sake of keeping up appearances. I know that it's ok to not be ok, and that plastering a brave face on when inside you are really struggling can be very detrimental. We should all be comfortable with sharing when things are wrong and not feel like we are being negative, being energy vampires, or pulling other people down. Equally though, we should be ok with being happy! I have sometimes found that I have felt almost guilty about being happy at times. Of course, when a friend or loved one is going through a difficult time, you aren't going to show up and start singing about how wonderful your own life is; but we should never feel bad because our own life **is** going well.

I knew that to focus on my own mindset and keep as positive as I could, I had to do a lot of different things.

I literally like to fill myself with positivity. It may sound difficult to do in a world which is filled with pain and suffering... but the truth is, you **do** have a choice in how much negativity you allow into your own life. As Louise Hay stated, "You are the only thinker in your own head". You get to choose your thoughts! Of course, the first thought which comes into your mind isn't always in your control as such, but you do have control over what comes **next**.

You **can** choose positive thoughts, instead of always allowing negative thoughts to rule you. Of course, this won't stop sad or bad things *happening*. It's not a cure for anything. It won't suddenly make the entire world a better place, **but** it will make **your** world a better place. It will help you deal with things differently, usually in a better way. It may help you stop worrying, or having imposter syndrome, or catastrophising quite as much. When you speak unkindly to yourself, your body will listen and put you into *dis-ease.*

It all starts with what you put into your mind. I have found that by choosing to opt out from watching the news or watching certain things on TV that aren't positive, not gossiping, not sitting dwelling on the past, or panicking about the future... my mindset has become a much better one. We are alone with our thoughts all the time. Our mind is our one constant thing with which we live ... so it's up to us to make sure it's a nice place to be.

I work on my mindset every single day... and I will continue to work on it every single day for the rest of my life. It's a lifelong commitment. One which I will never regret because not only does it help me, but it also helps all others around me. I know that when I am feeling negative, my whole demeanour changes. I am snappy and grumpy. I have less energy and I don't always want to be around people. Little things affect me and get me down. I struggle with simple things and feel overwhelmed easily. I basically feel pretty awful.

When I feel positive, my whole world changes for the better. It is well documented that the body and mind are linked, and I have certainly seen the truth in this during my illness and during my recovery too. Society now has us conditioned so that when we become unwell, we tend to seek help from the medicine cabinet; but we could do with looking inwards first. Illness is a way of our body trying to talk to us. Unfortunately, we have now become so busy with the hundreds of things we tell ourselves we **need** to do every day, that we usually don't allow ourselves the time to slow down, or even stop, and properly listen to our bodies and our minds. It has become faster and easier to simply mask over any issues with quick fixes.

When our body is diseased, the clue is in the title... *dis-ease.* The body is uneasy, it is telling us that something is wrong. Our mindset plays a huge part in how we deal with this. When our mindset is such that we tell ourselves that we 'haven't got the time to be unwell', we will keep pushing though. 'Soldiering on', 'Powering through', 'Can't keep me down', 'I don't have time to be ill'.... all phrases which are common now and we seem to wear them like a badge of honour. We think we are being strong by *battling* through illness. The sad thing is, if it was our child, parent or loved one who wasn't feeling well, we would be urging them to take some time out and get better... yet we often do the very opposite ourselves. It's no wonder that so many of us are struggling. When your body isn't well, how on earth can you expect your mind to be well?

When I decided to do whatever it took to try and recover from M.E. I knew that I had to stop and *listen* to my body and my mind. I had to stop **fighting.** Your body and mind don't want to fight you... they want peace. We all want peace, and yet we are often our own worst enemies. We fill our minds and bodies with junk... but expect them to keep performing optimally for us! All around us are phrases of us fighting... fighting the battle of illness, fighting with our own minds - and I fail to see how that does us any good. Mother Theresa famously said that she would never go to an 'anti-war' rally but would happily attend a 'pro-peace' one. That's how we should be thinking when we think of our ourselves. Not about us fighting, or battling, but learning to be at *peace* with ourselves.

Once I settled into the habit of listening to myself properly, I realised that all these horrible symptoms were here to try and get me to do exactly what I was being forced to do...to slow down. We weren't designed as humans to be doing the hundreds of things we now do each day. We are constantly multi-tasking, and we fail to focus on one thing at a time, because we are so very busy. We pride ourselves on how many things we can do each day, and often try to out-do each other in how many things we can get through all the time. We may look at people who do less than us with disdain and get fed up with our partners or family members if they are seen sitting down and taking time out for themselves, while we are busy running around like a headless chicken. We may sarcastically comment to others who are looking after themselves that it 'Must be nice to have time to yourself'. We can be envious of people who take the time to relax; yet, given the opportunity, we often fail to do it ourselves. It's like we are in competition with each other to see who can be the busiest! All of this will at some point lead to burnout.

Of course, everyone is different. We all have different levels of stress which we can deal with. We may feel that it is weak to accept help, or that we are showing ourselves up to be vulnerable if we can't fit everything in. We may secretly look down on others if they don't appear to have it all together... and so we may worry that other people will look down on us if *we* don't have it all together ourselves. Social media again doesn't help with this because it has become far easier to showcase what we do, and we can all compare ourselves to others and feel like we aren't enough. There's always that mum who seems to be perfect, or the dad who manages to work full time and help with football training, or the person running two jobs while raising a family and looking after their own parents, or the person who is achieving promotion after promotion in work, or the super athlete running six marathons in a day (OK, maybe that last one is an exaggeration and I may be touching on a sore point of mine, but you hopefully get the point I'm trying to make).

To be truly happy, we need to look after our bodies and our minds. You would think that with how much wellbeing is talked about now, it should be easy for us to do, and yet it isn't always that easy. We have become conditioned in a way that it's almost acceptable to fill ourselves with rubbish, both body and mind. Quite often, when people have decided to make their lives better in any way, they can be ridiculed, or told that they will probably fail. Ultimately, it doesn't matter what anyone else thinks though, it's all down to what **you** think. There comes a point in your life where you must be willing to take control of your own life. You must accept that if you aren't happy, it is **your** responsibility to do something about it. We can all play the victim card, because in all honesty, we have *all* had bad things happen in our lives. Again, we can play the comparison game here, and tell ourselves that our life is so much worse than somebody else's because we have been through so much more. The truth of it is that quite often, we may not be aware of what someone else has gone through, as not everyone talks about what has gone on. Even if you know for a fact that you have gone through more traumatic experiences than someone you know, that does not give you a reason/excuse to be more miserable than them. We all deal with things differently. Equally, we shouldn't be judging ourselves, or others, for dealing with something in a different way. Just because one person isn't affected by something you perceive to be awful, doesn't mean that you aren't validated in your own emotions around it.

What's true though is that while the world is full of suffering, it is also full of the overcoming of suffering. There are stories all around the world of people who have gone through truly horrific ordeals, and yet they have somehow turned their pain around and managed to not only survive, but indeed gone on to *thrive*. Victims of abuse, survivors of the holocaust, people who have suffered through war, people who have lost loved ones, survivors of true atrocities - so many people have gone through things which would for sure make so many people crumble... and yet they have gone on to live great lives and do amazing things.

So, if people can survive atrocities, and even go on to thrive following them, surely that is *proof* that our mindsets are a big part in helping us. When you choose to be a survivor and not play the victim, you are taking control of your own life and choosing happiness. You are in charge of your own well-being. You have **power**.

It's difficult, of course. But you never have to be alone. There are now more than ever, so many tools to help you cope. There are so many organisations which have been set up purely to help people. There are charities, groups, internet sites, communities...all designed to help people live their best life. It doesn't even have to cost a penny. A quick internet search will pull up thousands of things which can help anyone in pretty much any situation. The trick is to look for the help...and to accept it. Then, you get to work... on YOU.

The changes won't happen overnight. It takes time and effort, especially if you are coming from a background where you have been conditioned to not always focus on the good. With so much negativity around it, it can certainly be hard to suddenly try and live a more positive life. There will be barriers, and there are likely to be slip ups along the way. The thing is though, the stronger your mindset is though, the easier it will be to deal with difficult situations when they do come along.

We all know that we will have experiences which will hurt us in life. We all suffer losses. We all face rejections and humiliations. It's life. But we don't have to sit around and wait for them to happen. We don't have to invite them in. The quote which always makes me sad is when people say, 'Bad things always come in 3s'. Well, of course they will...because someone is actively putting it out there that they are *waiting* for something bad to happen. Plus, something which may not have bothered you too much, is likely to have a bigger impact if you put more onus on it being one of your 'bad things' which you have been expecting.

I am now a huge fan of affirmations (which I will discuss in more detail later) and really believe that the things you think and/or say have a huge impact on what is going on in your life. Of course, there are things which are out of your control... but there are also things which are **in** your control. One of those is the way you speak to yourself. If you are always being mean to yourself, how can you expect to be happy? It is so important that you instead speak to yourself as you would speak to someone you love... with love, kindness, and compassion. Again, this can be hard if you have spent a lot of your life being self-critical. It is so sad what we do to ourselves. We weren't born thinking anything horrible about ourselves, so something has changed along the way. We can choose to blame other people, and there can be no denying that other people's actions and words can play a huge part in how we think of ourselves, especially in our younger years. But at some point, you must decide that you are taking back *control* of your own mind. **You** choose how you think about yourself. **You** choose how you talk to yourself. **You** choose what you believe and don't believe. While other people can say things to you, it's up to **you** what you allow to have any control in your mind.

We spend so long trying to build other people up, especially children, and yet often fail to build the most important person up...YOURSELF! I know it can seem selfish and even big headed to build yourself up and take time for yourself... but the truth is quite the opposite. When you think about it, the happier you are as a person, the happier you are likely to make others around you. Think about the people you would prefer to spend your time with... are they happy and positive, or are they miserable and negative? Do you like hearing people put themselves down, or do you find it upsetting? Does it hurt you when you see people you love belittling themselves and choosing to ignore their own potential? Well guess what? Someone could be thinking that about you! The more you work on liking, or even better, loving yourself, the better it is for everyone around you. So, it's *far* from selfish because you are benefitting other people around you. You are making the world a nicer place to be in, because you are a nicer person. You being happy can make the world around you a happier place... that doesn't really sound selfish at all, does it?

One thing I know is that I will continue to work on my own mindset for the rest of my life. What started as a commitment for my own recovery, is now a lifetime practice. I will never go back, because to go backwards would be inviting bad health back in, both physically and mentally. It's a full commitment to **everything** I do to keep my mindset strong. I know that there will be days I may not want to do certain things. There may be days where I tell myself I'm too 'busy' to meditate, or I get to bed exhausted and realise I've forgotten to do any affirmations, or I will decide that having a few days of unhealthy eating will be fine, or I will want to watch the next series of something I used to watch, or I'll find myself getting sucked into the scroll hole on social media...and at that point I will have a choice. Of course, I will never beat myself up for small slips. I may have a few drinks on a special occasion **if** I feel like it. I may choose to watch something I wouldn't usually. I will even find myself rallying against myself and my positive attitude, because it will feel too damn hard to keep up. On those days I will remind myself that it's really a simple choice... **I get to choose illness or wellness.** While it may sound dramatic, I know that for me, it is true!

I know that even if I change one helpful thing for a day or two (or even a week or so), I must ensure that I keep on top of everything else I do and get back to doing everything as soon as possible. I won't ever be so structured that it makes me miserable... the things I do have quite the opposite effect to be honest. The things I do make me happy and healthy... and *keep* me healthy and happy. There is nothing I do which now feels like a massive effort, because I have incorporated everything into my life in such a way that it has become my 'norm'. I have changed my habits. I have stopped worrying about what people will think of me when I say I choose to do or not do a certain thing (food and alcohol are always an interesting one around other people as I've found others try to persuade you into having just one 'treat'). I don't feel like I'm missing out on anything in life, because my life now feels so rich. In fact, my life feels better than it did prior to me getting ill.

You often hear of people who have had a traumatic event happen in their life and they will say how it shaped them and made them a better person. They can even sometimes say they are grateful for what happened. I remember reading a book of recovery from M.E. stories and so many people were saying that they were grateful for getting ill, as it had eventually helped them change their lives for the better. I scoffed. In fact, it made me quite angry. I couldn't understand how anyone who had genuinely felt so horrific could now say that they were 'grateful' for that time in their life. It made me question how unwell they truly were (which is a horrible thing to do, given how many people with this illness aren't believed by other people... but I want to be as open and honest in this book as possible. I'm also pretty sure that I won't be the only ill person who has questioned somebody who has got better, because when you are so ill, you can find it impossible to believe that you may get better). I never imagined for a minute that I would be one of those people...but then I decided to set an intention. I decided that I wanted to be someone who could say that I was grateful. I wanted to **recover**. I wanted to get my life back.

One of the things I needed to learn was that I had to stop wanting the 'old me' back. The old me had become seriously ill. The old me was constantly busy and refused to take time out. The old me was self-critical and mean to herself. The old me didn't look after herself properly. The old me worried far too much about completely insignificant things. The old me pushed herself past the point of overwhelm because she refused to say no. The old me said yes to things which made her unhappy and said no to things she truly wanted to do. If I wanted *her* back, then I had to accept that at some point, I could be welcoming illness back in. I didn't want that... so I had to choose **me** over everything and everyone else.

I'm proud to now say that I **am** grateful for my M.E... because it has helped me find the real **me**. I know that there will be people reading this who will be doubting how ill I was, who may be comparing my illness to their own and saying that I obviously wasn't as bad as them (and that may even be true for some of you of course), and there will be people reading this and it could make you think I am crazy. There may even people who this will make them a little angry because it seems the most ridiculous thing to say (especially when you are deep in your own illness).

At one point I wouldn't have admitted to this gratitude because I was too worried about what people would say. Now... I don't care! Don't get me wrong, **I do** care about people! I care deeply. That's one of the reasons I'm taking the time to write this book. That's why I fill my social media feed with positivity. That's why I will still always do my best to be a good person and be available to help people. But the difference now is that I know that I cannot be responsible for what people think. Some people will take a long time to realise this, and some may never get it - but **you** are in control of your own life. You have the power to make changes in your life which will benefit you. Even if you are bed bound, or in horrific pain, or facing a terminal illness...you still get to choose how you **respond** to life and how you treat yourself. You can decide to live your best life no matter what life throws at you, or you can decide to complain about how life is treating you and do nothing about it. It may sound harsh, but again, it really is as simple as that!

The best thing about changing your mindset is that you can start right **now**! We are all guilty of putting things off. The diet starts on Monday... I will start exercising when it's better weather... I'll do a course when I can afford it... I'll leave my abusive partner when the kids have left. The list can go on. The truth is that the best time to start anything is always **now**! If you are telling yourself that you *can't* start this straightaway, you won't commit to yourself. You may not think you deserve a better life, and you may be frightened of making the changes. You may have tried to change something in the past and failed, and now you are telling yourself that you will probably fail again, so what's the point? You may be putting someone else first and thinking that you haven't got the time for changes! But truly, with mindset, you **can** start now! You can start now by telling yourself something good about yourself. You can start now by looking in the mirror and promising that you are committed to giving yourself a better life. You can start now by speaking to someone who you class as positive/helpful and getting some support. You can start now by deciding to cut negative things out of your life, maybe watching something positive to give you a boost. Just ***start***!

Throughout this book I will share in more detail the things which help me with my mindset and which I do daily. When I first started some of them, I thought they were a bit 'woo-woo' or told myself I was lying to myself so was unsure whether they would work... but I promise you everything I do **does** work towards making you healthier! As stated earlier, I am in no way an expert. I don't have any degree in how the mind works, so am not coming at you from a scientific or professional background. I doubt I will confuse you, as my writing is simple and plain. I will never say that if you do what I do, you will be 'cured' of anything. At the time of writing *this* section of the book, I would not say I'm fully recovered, but I do have confidence that one day I will be (who knows, maybe by the end of the book I will be able to say I am?), but what I am right now is healthier and happier than I have ever been. (EDIT... a year on, and I DO class myself as recovered. I treat myself very differently to how I used to though and believe that keeps me well.) I am at peace with myself. I am positive and upbeat - genuinely, rather than simply putting a brave face on. I feel I am a better role model to my children because I think about the things they hear and see me do, and I want them to grow up seeing positivity, kindness, and self-love.

I will not write about anything which I do not firmly believe in. I will never give medical advice of course as I am not a doctor, and I will **always** advise that anybody who is ill does go and see their own doctor and get diagnosed professionally. If you see a doctor and aren't happy with what they are saying, never be afraid of asking for a second opinion. It isn't about wasting time or hurting someone's feelings... it's about getting to the bottom of what may be wrong with **you**... and you matter! I will never promise that making these changes will be easy... but I do promise that they are worth it! Even if you only make one positive change in your life, that's a **huge** step and should be applauded! And you know, you *are* allowed to applaud yourself! It may seem strange at first but being your own best friend may be one of the best things you ever do for yourself!

Remember... you are wonderful! Life is amazing, even when it's really hard! Life loves you, so don't tell yourself otherwise... let's start as we mean to go on right?

TREATING RECOVERY AS A FULL TIME JOB

When I first became unwell, I fully expected to get better quickly. With hindsight, I can see that I did get ill more often than I would have liked to throughout my life (pre-M.E.), but I never stayed ill for too long. I remember at the start of my M.E. journey how I would go to bed every night thinking (and hoping) that tomorrow would be the day I felt better. I never would have believed that it would take years to get better! Even writing that, it seems almost impossible to think that it takes years for people to get better... and yet that's generally life with M.E.

I now know that I allowed myself to wallow for a long time. I felt really, really sorry for myself. I turned myself into a victim because of my illness. Of course, people will probably understand that, because being ill is simply horrible, and to be diagnosed with something which you get told by the medical experts is medically incurable and that you can expect to get worse - well, that's pretty difficult to get your head around. With the best will in the world, most people will feel sorry for themselves. It isn't just feeling sorry for yourself of course, it's fear. Genuine fear of whether you will *ever* get better. Concern about what the future will hold. Anxious thoughts about how your life will now turn out. Feelings of isolation as the world moves on without you. Loss of friends along the way. Loss of your purpose in life sometimes. It's no wonder so many people with M.E. go on to suffer with depression and other mental illnesses.

It can be difficult to motivate yourself to do the things which can help you to get yourself better. I'm aware that people may not understand this...but I can guarantee that most people in life will have something that they think/know they 'should' do, but they just don't! How many people don't exercise regularly, or choose to eat foods which they know may harm their bodies, or drink alcohol, smoke, take drugs, stay in toxic relationships, or get caught up in behaviour which makes them feel bad about themselves? Even though most of us **know** how we should be living in order to live our best lives...we quite often don't! It seems like it's easier to live a life which is quite detrimental to us, but which we have grown accustomed to! Change is difficult, even when it would massively benefit us.

When you are completely exhausted and in constant pain, along with all the other symptoms of M.E. it can be hard to become disciplined enough to do the things which will help you. Of course, everyone **wants** to be better, and lots of people will try lots of different things at different times... but it takes a lot of strength and dedication to really commit to yourself and do whatever it takes to aid your own recovery.

My husband James said to me after I received my official diagnosis, that I needed to make my recovery my full-time job.

Honestly... I was not prepared to do that at that particular time! It may sound daft (unless you can fully comprehend what goes on in situations like this), but I was still busy putting everyone else first. Putting **myself** first felt way too selfish. I was a mum, a wife, a daughter, a sister, an employee, a friend, a volunteer... how on earth could I fully commit to myself and make my recovery a full-time job without being utterly selfish?

However, once I realised that it was what I truly needed to do and started doing it, it was 100% the best thing I did for myself... and for my family! Once I accepted that without committing to myself and my recovery I would make myself worse, I realised that I would actually be benefiting my loved ones in the long run.

When I agreed to commit to my recovery plan for a minimum of six months, I told myself that those six months would pass anyway. They would either pass with me keeping on doing what I was already doing and expecting different results (which of course Einstein told us is the definition of insanity) or I could change things with the intention of fully committing to the changes and not stopping doing them within a few days/weeks/months simply because I wasn't seeing the results I wanted. We live in such a fast-paced world and want those 'instant results' or 'quick fixes'... and with this I had to accept that it wasn't possible! I knew I needed to put the work in. I had to put the work into **me**.

I drew myself up a recovery plan and I let the closest people around me know what was happening, so that I had support around me. I needed to know that everyone would help me on this journey as I anticipated that it would be hard. One quote I really love is 'Choose your hard', which I found to be very apt at this time. I needed to know that I had people who could help me. I needed people to make sure that I wouldn't push myself and so would intervene if necessary. I needed people to help me with the kids. I needed to know that someone wouldn't try to encourage me to veer away from my new eating plan. I needed people to talk to when extra support was necessary.

I had to say no. A lot. Saying no to people did not come easily to me. I had always prided myself on being the person who others could come to for help. I would make myself available for others as much as I could, even when it was to my own detriment! I had obviously had my life change so much that I had been forced to stop doing a lot and so had to say no to a lot of things already. But now I was making a conscious decision to start saying no more often, even if I felt I could/should be doing it. It even meant saying no to my children sometimes as I knew that I had to prioritise myself and so had to have more real rest. That was obviously hard, but I knew it was essential for my recovery.

Although I found it difficult to start saying no more, every time I did, I told myself that I was helping myself get better, and that really helped me mentally. I felt mean for saying no... but when I realised that I was being mean to *myself* if I kept saying yes to things which could end up making me more unwell, or to things I didn't truly want to do, then my attitude towards it all began to change. I saw that it was far better to say yes to the things I really wanted to do which made me happy personally, rather than say yes to things out of a sense of obligation, or even guilt. Don't get me wrong, I love helping other people, but there must be a limit! When your body talks to you and you have learned to listen, it becomes easier to connect and work out the things you genuinely want to say yes to.

I made myself rest much more. Proper rest of course. No TV, no phone, no social media, no reading... nothing which could distract me away from getting true rest. Sometimes I slept, and sometimes I simply allowed myself to fully rest. I meditated a lot more. The more I practiced the easier and more natural it became to do that and the quieter my mind got, which was amazing! My body responded well to it, and I realised that for the first time ever, I was practising real self-care. Even better, through the affirmations I was doing daily, I was starting to allow self-love too! This was so wonderful as I know now that my body had been starved of self-love for so long. I had spent so many years mentally beating my body up, ignoring its needs and pushing it, and it hadn't been given the love it deserved. I started to appreciate how wonderful my body was, even through the pain and suffering I was dealing with. I truly believe that this played a big part in my recovery. If you are constantly berating your own body, I feel sure that it has a negative effect on it. Thoughts turn into feelings and feelings become physical symptoms, so it makes sense that we really do affect how our body feels with what we are thinking and telling ourselves.

It felt strange. I knew I wasn't lazy, but sometimes I would worry that maybe I was being. It was hard accepting much more help and I worried that I was being a burden to other people. I wondered if I was a failure. But then... I worked hard on my mindset. I knew that recovering from this illness would be the **most** important thing I would ever do in my life. I knew that if I didn't commit to myself and do everything it took, then I would live to regret it. I knew that I could only be the mum/wife/friend/employee/volunteer I wanted to be, if I gave myself the best opportunity to get myself better. Every time any negative thought popped into my head, I chose to repeat the affirmations which were helping me get through, and to remind myself that I was doing the best I could. I remembered that as well as doing this for myself, I was doing it for my family and loved ones too.

I also realised that I had to stop wanting to be the 'old me'. There hadn't been anything 'wrong' with the old me of course. However, I truly believe that I became ill because my body was trying desperately to tell me things which I had refused to listen to. Eventually my body had forced me to stop so I had no choice but to listen. One day, after months of mindset work and with all the changes I had made, I suddenly had a bit of a lightbulb moment. I saw that the clue was in the initials of the illness. It was all about **me.** I hadn't been truly looking after *me*! Until I accepted the illness and accepted that it was on me to get myself better, then I may never do that. I realised that this wouldn't be a fast process. In fact, I accepted that this would be a lifetime of work. Initially this felt a little daunting... but when I sat and thought about it properly, I realised that it was amazing. I had been given this opportunity to make myself a priority and to really look after myself. I had the chance to truly learn about the person I was, and the person I wanted to be. It wasn't about getting better so that I could go back to the way I had been before I got ill, as that clearly hadn't been working for me. I could see that if I went back to being 100 miles an hour, I would risk becoming unwell again and may end up in an even worse position than I was now.

When you are ill, with absolutely anything, I truly believe that if you dedicate time to your recovery, you will get better much faster. I hear so many people saying the exact same thing as I used to..." I don't have time to be ill." People try to power through illness and somehow it seems like it's almost a sign of weakness if we 'give in' to illnesses. It is as though the world expects us to struggle through! It's never helpful to our bodies to do that! Comparison can rear its ugly head again here too, as we may look around at other people who are unwell and still managing to do a hundred things. We can think that if they are carrying on, then surely we should too. The worst thing you can do is compare yourself in this way. Take the time to stop and listen to **your** body! Let your body tell you what to do, rather than another person or your sense of obligation! There truly is only ever so much that your body and mind can take before an inevitable crash in some way. Even if you are dealing with a cold, it's important to take the time to properly look after your body! Of course, I'm not saying you need a week off work for a slight cold... but a bath, some nourishing food and an early night will work far better than watching crap TV, eating junk food, and staying up late and being on your phone half the night will ever do!

I fully appreciate that there will be people reading this who think that they would love to have the opportunity to treat their recovery as a full-time job, but they simply can't, for a variety of different reasons. It may be that you may not **have** to treat it as a full-time job if your symptoms haven't taken over your life. For me, I ended up feeling like I had no choice because M.E. had robbed me of so many things and I did not want to end up fully bed bound... and unfortunately that was the way we saw it going if I did not make the full commitment to myself. However, if your symptoms allow you to still work and/or partake in other activities, but you are really struggling, then I would advise that you take a good look at what you **can** do to help yourself. I in no way mean to sound patronising or disrespectful to anyone, and I know from experience how truly devastating this illness is, even in its mildest forms, but I really believe that to recover properly, you need to be prepared to make your recovery the most important thing. This may mean making certain changes which mean that other people will be affected. It may mean reducing work hours, it may mean getting more help from other people, it may mean paying people to do some jobs for you (if you can afford it), it may mean saying no much more when people ask you to do things.

For me, making the conscious decision to treat my recovery as a full-time job helped me to change my mindset about it all. Rather than telling myself I was pathetic or lazy for needing to rest, I told myself that it was part of my **job**. I was so much kinder to myself when I took the time to look after myself, knowing that it was an essential part of my 'job'. My goal was to get better and that meant putting my effort into doing the necessary things to ensure that would happen, as opposed to wasting energy on putting a brave face on through it all and pretending I was far better than I really was.

When you treat something as a job, it can really help you get in a frame of mind which builds determination. Ultimately, your recovery be for everyone's benefit, especially yours, and so committing to yourself will be the best thing you can do.

DIET

This is an area of my recovery which usually generates a lot of interest, even with people who aren't ill themselves. It's one thing which people who know anything about nutrition will try to fully attribute my recovery to... or it's what people ask me about when they realise I lost all of the three plus stone I put on since my illness in under six months... or they want to know how I actually *do* it with all of the changes I have made.

It is what I tend to get a little bit anxious about when I talk about to be completely honest, because I feel quite passionate about it. Not as passionate as I do about mindset (which I will always attribute to being the main thing which helps anyone with anything), but still pretty passionate. Mainly because I feel that the word 'diet' is so misused, and I think that so many people are so concerned nowadays about weight loss/gain and how their body looks... rather than the actual health of their body.

I will state right now that I'm not able to give professional nutritional advice so please do not expect that. I will always advise that anyone looking to make serious dietary changes for their health should seek appropriate advice from professionals. While I do have a degree in Food and Nutrition, I have never done anything with it professionally and so the advice I offer here is mainly from what I have learned during my illness through research done for my own recovery.

Food and my 'diet' have always been a pretty big thing for me... mainly because **I really** love food, and because I was very, *very* greedy! Growing up, I was skinny, and I absolutely hated it. I would get teased for being skinny. I vividly remember crying to my mum one day, I think I must have been about 10, wishing that I could be fat as I figured it would be easier to lose weight than it would be to put it on. I had no idea.

We had a fairly good diet at home growing up. Nutrition wasn't really the buzzword it is today, and convenience foods were becoming more popular. We would always start the day with a bowl of cereal or porridge, or a piece of toast; school dinner, or a sandwich if we were at home- and then our evening meal. Then snacks consisting of fruit, crisps, biscuits, chocolate... the usual kinds of foods most of us probably grew up with.

When I went to secondary school, and got more independence with how I ate, I chose poorly. I would have breakfast at home; crisps for morning break; lunch/dinner would be a portion of chips and gravy with a barmcake, followed by some sort of chocolate covered treat afterwards. Then, because I always had dinner money left over, since I hadn't had a proper meal at lunchtime, I would walk to the local shop on the way home and buy myself a chocolate bar. Might not sound too bad... but this was every day. Also, it wasn't just any chocolate bar. I would buy myself a 200g bar of Dairy Milk, which I would eat on the way home, so that my mum didn't know what I had done. The shop was halfway up my street... so I gobbled that chocolate fast! This habit lasted for years!

I stayed slim. People would see me eat and be amazed at how much I could put away without gaining a lot of weight. As I got older, I realised that far from being teased for that, it was something to be envied. As I watched girls around me starting diets and denying themselves certain foods, I was doing the opposite. I was a little obsessed with food. During my teenage years I would spend any pocket money I had at the weekend on junk food. I had a paper round from being 13 and all the money I earned went on snacks. When I think back, I genuinely can't believe how much harm I put my poor body through with the foods I chose.

I was still eating three meals a day each day, as well as almost constantly snacking. Once I discovered alcohol... well, that opens a whole new world with your dietary health, right?! I would be going out a couple of nights a week when I turned 18, drinking, eating fast food at 2am, getting up and having an unhealthy breakfast and getting through the day on unhealthy snacks.

To my shame, even when I was at university, studying Food and Nutrition I was still throwing junk in my body. Grabbing something at the train station, getting a sandwich and chocolate for lunch, an unhealthy snack in the afternoon, something else on the journey home, tea and then more snacks. Caffeine would help to keep me awake... thrown in with my weekends of partying and eating more and more junk.

I do know that I'm not alone in eating like this. It's become easier and easier to eat processed food, and it's harder in a lot of ways to prepare good, healthy wholesome food. We are surrounded by heavily processed food. It's advertised everywhere, it's quick, cheap and highly addictive! It's been *designed* to be addictive! Companies spend big money on making these foods addictive and making sure that they are heavily advertised so that we see them and immediately want them.

I can guarantee that you could probably think of ten heavily processed foods or restaurant's logos or jingles off the top of your head (go on... sing out loud the one which is in your mind). Yet, I bet you can't think of many adverts for fresh fruit and vegetables. "A visit to the greengrocers makes your day" never quite took off the same way another song did (and if you're now thinking about a certain food because of a jingle in your head while reading this, and possibly now want that particular food, it just goes to prove how powerful these messages truly are).

This way of eating continued for pretty much all my adult life, until I got ill. My body didn't stay the same, and while I have been blessed to never have to have serious weight battles to deal with, I certainly put weight on over the years.

I have always exercised though, so usually managed to maintain a healthy weight.

When I was pregnant with my first born, Jack, I put on a whopping six stone! I had been warned by my consultant to not exercise while I was pregnant due to some issues I had. On top of not exercising, I absolutely ploughed through food. I told myself that 'baby wants it'... while I would destroy a full birthday cake or block of cheese!

I told myself that I have never believed in yo-yo dieting as I am well aware of the havoc it can cause on your body, and your mental health. I never considered myself as being on a 'diet' when I wanted to lose weight previously, I would simply follow a good healthy eating plan in some ways for a set time. It wouldn't take long though, until I was back on to my beloved chocolate, crisps, cakes, biscuits, alcohol, pasta dishes, chippy teas...you name it, I would eat it! It has only been while writing this that I've had to accept that even though I prided myself on not ever 'dieting', I actually *did* follow the classic 'yo-yo' dieting pattern. I hate the term, so it's been a real eye opener to discover this about myself and be able to admit to it.

I would tell myself that I was healthy... and while I refuse to beat myself up about this as I believe that would be more detrimental, I know that I wasn't really that healthy at all. While I **did** have a fairly balanced diet in some ways, in that I always drank plenty of water, ate ok amounts of fresh fruits and vegetables and would eat a variety of foods... my processed foods intake was high. Even though I home cooked a lot of food for my family, I would quite happily reach for a jar of processed pasta or curry sauce. I was a busy mum, and used the viable excuse of 'Who has time to prepare fully home cooked food'? Almost every parent knows the feeling of utter frustration when you do make something from scratch... then the kids refuse to eat it and ask for toast instead! It's unlikely to encourage you to cook freshly prepared meals.

I hadn't really taken a good look at what I was actually eating, because I guess I didn't really feel I needed to. I was slim, and maybe that helped me in my belief that I was healthy enough. I didn't have any major worries with pain or anything else, so figured I was doing just fine.

Except... if I had truly looked, I would have seen that actually I **wasn't** quite as fine as I liked to tell myself. I was tired. A lot. **Not** like M.E. tired (you simply can't compare any kind of tiredness to that and to do so is quite insulting). I felt and looked tired though. I woke up tired, stayed tired all day and went to bed tired. But it was the kind of tired that I think most people can understand. It's a general lethargy. One that we see as being the 'norm' nowadays, because we are all so damn busy. We rarely switch off, and with how obsessed we have become with our phones, the 'busyness' can start as soon as we wake up, and not finish until we go to sleep. So I didn't see this tiredness as anything to worry about. I got through it with sugar and caffeine... again, probably the way most of us do without realising the damage we are doing to ourselves living like his.

Although I didn't really have any pain, I never really felt great either. It was all a bit... meh. My immune system wasn't great, and I would often pick up bugs and end up with a cold or chest infection etc. My periods were awful. My body was just kind of going through the motions. Surviving, but not especially thriving. I would push my body with exercise and work...and then fill it up with copious amounts of unhealthy foods - and tell myself that this was ok. I lived for food 'treats' without realising that my poor body was crying out for me to stop polluting my body with all these processed foods which weren't doing me any good.

I was treating my tastebuds... but not my body.

I heard a saying recently which I love. It is 'If you eat for health, you will never need to diet.' How true is that?! If you were being true to yourself and eating the foods which you knew were genuinely good for you, you wouldn't have to worry about 'dieting'. Your body would become its natural weight without having to feel starved!

When I got ill, I massively resisted changes to my diet. So whenever anybody asks me about my diet and I tell them what I now eat and don't eat, I know that a lot of them may reply with the same things I used to say.

"I couldn't cut out sugar/caffeine/alcohol/gluten/processed foods" ...one or all of these are usually stated.

"I could never have your self-discipline."

"I would feel like I had no fun in my life if I couldn't eat/drink exactly what I wanted."

"I couldn't cope going out anywhere and not being able to eat the food there."

"I could probably do it for a little while, but not forever!"

"Eating like that would just make me miserable."

"Eating is one of my only pleasures in life, I would feel awful if I lost out on eating as well." (This one is especially pertinent for people who are unwell and have had other things taken away like I had... job, exercise, social life etc).

"I don't have the time/energy to make food from scratch."

"Healthy food is more expensive than processed food and I can't afford such drastic changes."

"I would love to eat more healthily but the rest of the family won't eat what I would cook and I'm not making different meals."

"I would just miss a particular food too much."

"I've actually tried cutting out gluten/sugar/alcohol etc once and didn't really notice a massive difference, so I don't think it really works for me."

"I don't want to be a pain/burden to other people, so I'll just carry on the way I am so as not to cause disruption."

"I don't really enjoy fruits and vegetables. I don't like the healthier versions of other foods either... so it's not for me."

"It's great that it's worked for you... but I doubt it would work for me. My symptoms/situation/issues are different to yours."

"I wouldn't know where to start."

"I don't really enjoy cooking so don't fancy making a whole load of new recipes."

"I just don't want to change!"

Ok... so if you're reading through this list and find that you can relate to one (or more... even a lot more) of these comments, please know you are not alone! I pretty much said **every** single one of these comments myself on my path to recovery, so I do know how it feels to have those inner battles when it comes to food.

Initially, I didn't want to make the changes which I knew were necessary. Don't get me wrong... I wanted to get **better.** I just wanted there to be an easy way to do it. Ideally, I wanted there to be a way which still allowed me to eat chocolate, stuff my face with pizza and enjoy as much alcohol as my body could handle.

I was cross that I was ill, and I found some comfort in food. Deep down, I knew that the foods I was choosing to eat were harming me. There's no way devouring a huge bar of chocolate and munching through three packets of crisps, while necking a gin and tonic... all after my tea, could be doing me **any** good. Yet I persisted. I would fib to myself that I wasn't doing too badly as I was still eating fruit and vegetables, still drinking loads of water and having supplements just in case I was missing out on anything important. I would even play the comparison game. I would look at what other people were eating/drinking and reassure myself that at least I wasn't eating that way. Or I would look at people who had an ultra-healthy diet and still become unwell... so surely there was the proof that I needed that actually a really healthy diet couldn't be all that it was cracked out to be. (Many of us may choose to cling to hearing that minority story of someone who gets ill even though their diet/lifestyle is good... as it gives us that seal of approval for our own choices.)

During my illness, I had, of course, tried different ways of eating. I had periods where I would cut out gluten, or sugar, or alcohol, or dairy for a while. It would only ever be one thing at a time as I couldn't imagine doing more than one... never mind doing it all at once. I had lovely friends send me over recipes...not realising that the energy needed to even consider standing up in the kitchen to cook, never mind cooking a new recipe with lots of unknown ingredients, just wasn't there! I was exhausted even thinking about changing my diet and that exhaustion led to being more upset... which, in turn, led to me eating more junk food to try and get that comfort from it. It truly was a horrible cycle to be in.

When anybody asks me about my diet and replies with any of the comments I have previously mentioned, I can definitely relate to them. At one point (before I had worked **so** hard on my mindset) I would have tried to persuade someone to my way of thinking and implored them to make the changes. Not now. While I am more than happy to offer advice when asked for it (and part of my reason for writing this book is to get all that advice down in written format) I always try to assure people that any changes made must be right for them. I believe that when the time is right (and mainly when you have your mindset right, and you have enough of a desire to want to **truly** change) then you **will** do what is best for you. This may mean making one small change, or it may mean making many. I always think it is better to make changes that you are happy with and likely to stick to, rather than trying something without the right mindset, end up giving up, then feeling like a failure for not seeing it through. It's so important to be kind to yourself… and that certainly includes the diet choices you make.

When I had my really awful week and decided to commit to myself and my recovery, I finally accepted that my diet had to have a huge overhaul! I didn't want to play small, or just try a couple of things and then end up giving up. I knew that I was committing to a solid six months, where I could choose to either try my hardest to recover and feel better knowing that I had done this, or else I could give up and always wonder what could have been if I had been truly dedicated. Dedicated to my own wellness.

I had a few things which I said (and still say) which really helped me during this time. I knew that the food changes would be difficult (or at least, I expected them to be) and I knew I had to keep in my mind my WHY. Why was I doing this? Why was I willing to 'give up' all the foods I loved? Why was I willing to risk the possibility of being more miserable because I was likely to miss my favourite foods? Why was I ok with accepting that I may be more of a burden to people with my new diet? Why was I willing to spend more money, time and energy on new things, which I wasn't even sure I would like?

My **why** was strong. Thankfully it was (and still is) strong enough to see me through all the difficult patches when all I wanted to do was stuff my face with chocolate, or sink a glass (ok, bottle) of fizz. My why was **me**. Me and my family. I wanted to be well. I wanted to pain free. I wanted to enjoy my life properly again. I wanted to be able to go for a walk, or work again, or even get to the toilet without having to ask James to take me on my bad days. I wanted to enjoy my food of course… but I wanted to be able to cook it without having to go straight to bed, or to be able to eat it without my husband cutting it up for me or having to put my head down on the table to eat because it was too exhausting to sit up for too long. I wanted to look forward to going out for a meal and enjoying my food, rather than going out and being in so much pain that I couldn't enjoy what I was eating because I was trying so hard to simply not burst into tears. One of my biggest why's was wanting my children to stop believing I was dying. It was so that I wouldn't keep putting weight on, which was going to lead to even more health problems for me. It was because me being well was more important than me being ill. **I was choosing me, over M.E.**

I appreciate that this may sound quite harsh. People may feel I'm being judgemental; or that I'm implying that people choose to stay ill rather than get better. I'm certainly not being purposely judgemental. We all have our own journeys to travel, and we all have things we struggle with, which nobody should judge us for. Genuinely, there may be people who will change everything in their lives but still stay unwell. However, I will stand by the fact that I believe that when you do make important changes, it is more than likely that your health will improve. Mindset truly is the main thing which needs to be good... because when it is, sorting your diet and lifestyle becomes so much easier (and enjoyable too).

The changes in my diet seemed really difficult at first. Thankfully now I don't feel they are! I think that's because I truly believe in the changes I have made, and I have seen so many benefits. Also, because I still get to enjoy food a lot! I don't fuss about portion size. I feel full after the meals I eat (which was a big concern for me). I don't comfort eat (I won't lie, of course there are still times where I feel like I want to! 40-year habits are hard to break). I don't spend hours slaving in the kitchen making concoctions (ironically, I enjoy cooking more than I ever have done, but I'm not one for creating my own recipes! There won't be a cookbook coming out from me any time soon). When people sometimes balk when I tell them what I do and don't eat, I don't let it bother me anymore. I used to! I used to feel that I was being awkward, or a bit weird, or that people would look at me and think differently of me now that I was refusing to eat the cake and drink the wine. I have had people tell me that life is too short to not eat a particular food... but I believe that life is too short to spend it riddled with horrific pain! For me now, it's a much easier choice.

I simply choose wellness over illness.

My dietary changes included cutting out several foods. When I first started, I was **very** strict with myself for the first six months. I wanted to know that I was giving myself the best chance and giving everything a chance to work.

I cut out all refined sugar and artificial sweeteners. I cut out caffeine. I cut out gluten and most wheat products. I cut out practically all dairy, other than a bit of cheese. I cut out all alcohol. The drinks I chose to have daily were water and herbal teas. I stopped eating **all** highly processed foods.

Ok, so looking at that, you are either thinking, that doesn't sound too bad. Or you are thinking, that sounds horrible and unsustainable! I personally would have never believed that I could make the changes I did at one point – but I did, and so I know that these changes are possible!

The biggest change (and food challenge) for me was sugar. I was a complete sugar addict. Even now I am amazed with myself that I have managed to do what I have done, given how much sugar I used to consume! It's so hard when we are surrounded by sugary snacks everywhere we go... and even harder when you realise how much sugar gets added into products you wouldn't even think had it in!

Sugar gives us energy of course... but other than that it has absolutely no nutritional value. I would go so far as to say that sugar is making (and keeping) us ill. So many of us are probably addicted to it, with or without realising it, as it's become such a huge part of our daily food choices. Even if you aren't picking up lots of sugary snacks, the chances are that your intake of sugar will still be high if you are eating processed foods. Take a quick peek at the labels of most processed foods and you will often find sugar on there. You may be surprised at how high up it is in the ingredients list too! (The food manufacturers have got crafty and have come up with over 80 alternative names for sugar so people may not always realise that it has sugar in it!)

To my mind now, there is truly nothing good about sugar. Of course, it tastes good, and it makes other foods taste good. It may make that cup of coffee taste even better. As Mary Poppins so eloquently sings, it certainly helps the medicine go down (many a time I would have just a little bit of Calpol myself when giving it to the kids... I'm sure I'm not alone there). But what good is it doing to our bodies? I know that there will be people who claim that sugar is a necessity for them. Maybe it gives you an extra boost when you are struggling through the day. Maybe you are about to do exercise and need that extra energy at a specific point. Maybe it's the only way you can encourage your child to eat other foods (oh yeah... been there, done that).

Ultimately, I'm not here to try and make you do or give up anything you don't want to... I'm simply letting you know what has worked for me, and what is working for so many people who are giving up refined sugar and artificial sweeteners.

Sugar does give us a huge energy boost and delivers it fast. When we are feeling tired during the day at any time, it's easy to grab something sugary which we know will pick us up. Plus, it's delicious! We get a feel-good factor when we are eating it (although there are many people who will feel guilty after, or even during eating it which totally ruins any feel-good factor). Of *course* that's going to be a hard habit to kick! Even though we can probably tell that we are in a cycle where we feel tired, grab some sugar, slump after the energy runs out so we grab another sugary snack. It's hard to break that pattern.

Even when we fully *know* about how harmful sugar is to us, it can **still** be hard to give it up! Sugar has become an acceptable addiction; in fact, we even joke about it! Most of us wouldn't want to admit to being addicted to drugs, alcohol or medication... and yet we have no problem in laughing off the fact that we couldn't give up chocolate, or whatever sweet thing we are partial to. In fact, we are even encouraged to eat sugary things with adverts, promotions, TV, posters and even 'positive' quotes telling us that it's more than ok to give in to eating chocolate. How often do we see signs telling us to eat cake? Or watch films where people get stuck into a huge tub of ice cream when something bad happens to them. How often do we reward ourselves, and others with a sugary treat... yet we wouldn't dream of rocking up with a bag of cocaine for someone's birthday?! (And if you have gasped a bit at that last comment and think I'm taking a little bit far, research does show that sugar can be as addictive as opioid drugs. Sugar releases dopamine, eating it causes similar effects to how the brain reacts when substances such as heroin and cocaine are taken!) We can easily become addicted to the good feelings which we have when we eat sugar and because it is seen as being completely acceptable, we are unlikely to feel bad about our consumption of it.

I genuinely believe that cutting out refined sugar and artificial sweeteners has had the biggest effect for me diet wise. It's probably been the most difficult thing I've done because I had conditioned myself to become so used to eating it... and I loved it **so** much! But without doubt, it will have seen the biggest health benefits for me from a nutritional point of view.

I am well aware that avoiding **all** sugar is actually really hard to achieve, even with a balanced diet. I do still have fruit; and of course, fruits and other carbohydrates are converted into sugar in the body. So it would be easy to think that there's no point cutting it out, because your body will still be getting sugar. But that's just something you will tell yourself to make you feel better about eating sugar. Please don't get me wrong and think I am being patronising. Again, I know how very difficult this is to do! I have spent years, decades even, telling myself the exact same things, so I'm not coming from a 'holier than thou' place at all. I've struggled with this for so long! Honestly, without having made the changes in my mindset, I do not believe I could have done it. Willpower is great, but usually only gets you so far. There will always be a time where even the best will in the world hits a stumbling block which is just too much. That's where mindset comes in to remind you of your **why**! If you don't have a strong enough why, things are even more difficult. Getting down to your why will help you so much!

We have all heard, and possibly experienced, the withdrawal symptoms when you try to give up sugar (again, proof that sugar is addictive). Your body starts craving it or starts craving other things. You can get headaches, you may feel sick, you get grumpy. This may be enough to put you off doing it. But those feelings don't last forever (and when you're honest with yourself, you **do** know that they won't). The benefits you will see when you go sugar free will far outweigh feeling a bit rubbish for a week or two. (I do appreciate that the thought of feeling extra rubbish when you are already so unwell is a tough one to deal with... but it will always be worth it for the results you get after.)

I found it difficult at first when I looked at the foods I ate and saw how much added sugar there was in so many things. I knew that I would have to cut out cakes, biscuits, chocolate etc, but I hasn't realised quite how much was in other foods. It meant cooking more meals from scratch, which can be difficult. Time, money and energy constraints can really cause issues with this. Plus, I didn't really enjoy cooking, so it wasn't like I was all geared up for a new challenge. I wanted to cry. In fact, I did cry - quite a lot! I had to accept that I was going to have to live a new life, one where

I wouldn't automatically reach for chocolate when times were tough. I wouldn't enjoy a can of Fanta when it was hot, join the kids in ice cream or even eat a piece of birthday cake. I would no longer grab a jar of pasta sauce to add to meat for a quick spaghetti Bolognese. At times, all of that seemed to outweigh the goodness I knew I would be giving myself.

Food has become such an integral part of our social lives. We don't just eat to survive now. We eat for pleasure. We go out for meals. We have takeaways. We eat when we go to see a movie or a show. We have pizza nights at home, and most of our celebrated holidays revolve around food! Easter, Christmas, Valentine's Day, Pancake Day, Halloween, as well as birthdays and other family celebrations... all have become synonymous with sweet treats!

Making drastic changes in your 'diet' certainly requires a good mindset. It can be so easy to slip back into old habits of eating. We are surrounded by food, and we need it to survive. We have become so busy in our daily lives that while we love eating food, we may not always feel that we have the time to prepare good food. It's much easier to grab something quick, which is often pumped full of sugar and artificial ingredients, whilst also being devoid of nutrients. We shove readymade meals into microwaves and call out for unhealthy take aways. We often prefer white rice, pasta and bread rather than the (usually) healthier wholemeal versions, because our tastebuds have changed so much. Quite often, we don't have enough knowledge of the foods we are eating. Although most foods, and all processed foods now have nutritional labels on, we aren't all experts in reading them. The UK government 'kindly' gave us traffic light systems but unless you are well versed in nutritional knowledge, even they can be misleading. You may see something and assume it is healthy because it is colour-coded green for some things, but that will in no way mean that what you are eating is 'healthy'.

Companies spend so much money on advertising and marketing, making it so that we are drawn to particular foods. Foods are made to become almost addictive. Ingredients are added to foods to make us want more of them within a short period of time. Most scarily, companies are targeting children at a much earlier age. I remember hearing people say that they were buying their children a particular fruity ribbon like sweet (I had better not say the brand) as an alternative to fresh fruit, because they believed that they were a healthy option, due to its name. They didn't realise that actually, they are sweets! It's hard when you are dealing with situations like this as it is perfectly understandable why so many people would assume this, given that the name 'fruit' is on the label. The younger you are when you start eating unhealthy foods, the harder it usually is to stop! People fall into the habit of believing that to eat healthily is expensive... when in fact that is not necessarily true. When you fill yourself with proper, wholesome food which is not ram packed full of artificial additives, you will eat far less and eventually save yourself money. It is a shame of course than when we look in a shop, a chocolate bar may appear to cost less than a healthy alternative but when you do start to research it all properly, you will end up spending more on junk food if you are choosing to eat that way.

If you are thinking about making changes to your own diet, I can certainly recommend that you do some research into the foods you are currently eating. You may be amazed when you look at what ingredients make up your favourite foods. I'm not going to pretend that making drastic changes is easy... it really isn't. Having a family, I have struggled with making these changes because I know that not all of my family want to eat the same way I do. It's a tough one, because even though I know that the way I am eating would be better for all of us and so it should be simple, it hasn't been that simple in practice... so trust me when I say I get it. My kids have grown up having takeaways, going to fast food chains, having sweets, chocolates, white bread etc... and it's hard getting them to change overnight (they **have** eaten healthy meals too of course). I know it's easier for me because my health truly does depend on it... in a much more obvious way than theirs does currently. They won't potentially end up in bed for a week if they fill their body with junk... the same goes for my husband. When you love certain foods, it can be difficult to give them up. We are getting there slowly but surely. As chief cook in the house (again, this is another achievement as I had to give up this role during my illness), of course I have the last say in what we eat as a family, and I don't want to be making separate meals all the time, so there has been a bit of give and take... but we are certainly not a family who all eat fully the same (**yet**...she says hopefully).

What I really want to do is educate my children. I want them to make their own choices so that they can see what is good for their body, and what isn't so good... and hope that they can make the healthier choices. I think that's all we can ever do really. Part of the issue is when we don't know what is good for us. The way that certain foods are portrayed makes it difficult to know what is good for us at times. Years ago, fat was the enemy and everyone who wanted to get healthy and/or lose weight went on drastic fat excluding diets! Low fat foods became very popular... without people realising that in place of the fat- sugar, sweeteners and other unhealthy alternatives were pumped into the foods, which caused even more damage.

While I don't want to make this a strict section on what to eat and what not to eat, I do know that it can be hard when you start looking at how you can implement major dietary changes so will offer some advice and talk a bit about what I do eat.

As I have already stated, I cut out all refined and artificial sugar/sweeteners. I also tend to avoid natural sugars such as honey.

I cut out all gluten which can be much easier now with so many alternatives. **However**, I have found that a lot of the alternatives may contain ingredients I want to avoid (just to make it that bit tricker) so I do prefer to make my own things. I did buy gluten free bread occasionally at the start of changing over, but I make my own bread now if I ever want it. It's very different, of course, I can't deny that! But I have come to really enjoy the foods I make now. My tastebuds have changed quite a lot so very sweet things no longer taste as nice as they used to. Plus, the knowledge that I'm filling myself with good foods that won't be making me ill is a **big** part of how enjoyable something is.

I try to have vegetable alternatives (courgette spaghetti) rather than gluten free pasta, but again, will have the gluten free or wholemeal versions if necessary. Rice is either wholemeal or made from cauliflower.

I avoided dairy (other than cheese) for the first six months after some research led me to believe that would be best for me. I did (and still do) have cheese daily with my eggs and vegetables. My dairy intake is lower than what it used to be, and I think that works well for me. I understand for a lot of people going dairy free makes hugely positive changes for them, so would definitely say it may be worth giving it a try to see if it works for you. (I have chosen to re-introduce more dairy into my diet following my recovery, but it is something that I am currently monitoring.)

I am not vegan or vegetarian. I have considered it, but don't feel it's right for me, at this point. I do eat meat and fish, and especially love fish. Everything is a personal choice and I've researched all the pros and cons to eating meat versus not eating it, including all the animal welfare/climate change issues. I have been vegetarian years ago and I would consider it in the future if I felt it was right for me personally. I know now that nutritional knowledge is so important on many dietary changes you are looking at making... as you need to be sure that you are getting the right nutrients for your own body and health needs. We do choose to eat vegetarian and /or vegan meals during the week and have been steadily increasing this during my recovery.

I eat a lot of vegetables, nuts and seeds. I try to make sure I have vegetables in every meal of the day, even breakfast! At first, I couldn't imagine having vegetables for breakfast as it just didn't seem right, but now I absolutely love my scrambled eggs and veg dish. In fact, I love it so much I have it almost every day! James asked me recently if I wasn't bored of it, but I'm really not! I cook vegetables in coconut or extra virgin olive oil (usually spinach, kale, tomatoes, mushrooms, red onions and peppers), along with some nuts and seeds (currently pumpkin seeds, linseed, sunflower seeds, sesame seeds, pine nuts and chai seeds), add some Himalayan salt and pepper, then scramble a couple of eggs into it. I usually add a bit of feta cheese in there too! Yum! I tend to do my food preparation in one go each week, so that I have all my vegetables chopped up and in boxes for the week so that I can just chuck it all in.

I have a fruit and vegetable smoothie every day. Smoothies are a bit controversial as obviously they are blitzing foods which would be far better to eat naturally, but I believe that they have helped me. There are so many different things that you can put in there. My favourite one (which, again, I tend to stick to) has water, a banana, some frozen berries, spinach, kale, cucumber and then some superfood powders in (I choose to have maca powder, baoab, acia berry, wheatgrass, turmeric, collagen and chlorella... I buy them in bulk bags to save money and once a week I put them all into little pots so that I can just pop them into my blender). (I do appreciate that this is all extra cost... however I figure that I'm also saving money by not buying processed foods (which never filled me anyway.)

Lunches tend to be salads, stir fries (I make it with coconut oil which gives it a good flavour as I don't use a sauce, I make it very simply with vegetables and usually prawns), home-made soups, or (occasionally) jacket potatoes (another one people ask me, whether I eat white potatoes. I didn't for a while, but I do now),

I am a fan of intermittent fasting and practice it regularly one way or another. Intermittent fasting is where you only eat for a set amount of hours in the day. Without realising it, most of us do this anyway, as we don't eat while we are asleep! However, you can take it a step further and choose to 'fast' for longer. I tend to do this a few times a week after researching the benefits of it and realising that it made sense for me personally. (I will reiterate that what I am saying in this book is in no way medical advice and while I found this worked/works for me during my recovery, it may not be suitable for everyone, and I would recommend seeking professional advice.) It made sense for me to try it when I thought about how much energy the body uses in digesting food. I was at home more or less all of the time, and my eating was probably getting out of hand. I was definitely comfort eating, and I certainly wasn't sticking to 3 meals a day. I was having so many snacks... and my body was constantly expending energy digesting all that food. I reasoned that actually, if I made it easier on my body by not eating that way, I should end up having more energy available for the other activities I wanted to be doing. More importantly, my body would have more energy available to heal itself better. I started eating my evening meal a bit earlier and then making sure I didn't eat anything after that meal. The next day I would wait until lunchtime to eat. I found this difficult at first, but I was genuinely surprised at how quickly I got used to it... and how quickly my body adapted to it, and it felt right for me. My almost constant eating was a habit which I needed to break. Initially I told myself that I was making myself miserable at times, when I felt as if I was 'denying' myself of something I loved... but then I remembered my **why**. Why was I doing this? I was doing this to make my life better of course, and that had to be better than anything I could snack on all day would taste or make me feel.

If I am doing intermittent fasting, then I tend to have my eggs/vegetables concoction with my smoothie for lunch (and make sure I drink plenty of water (I try to have cooled boiled water) all morning).

Tea consists of a good variety of meals. I genuinely don't feel cheated or that I'm missing out on anything. We have adapted lots of things. We have probably gone back to eating the more traditional British way of eating meat/fish, potatoes and veg! Prior to starting my recovery journey, we ate a lot more pasta and rice dishes than we do now... although they do still form a staple part of our meals, just with alternatives, as I will have courgette spaghetti and cauliflower rice.

I stopped drinking alcohol. I thought that 'giving up' would be difficult if I'm honest. It almost feels shameful to say that because it may make you wonder whether I had a problem with alcohol. I genuinely don't think I did... but I did love a drink. During the Covid lockdown, we ended up drinking a lot more than we usually would. I was normally a social drinker, but lockdown had us drinking in the garden more. While I knew that I could give it up when I wanted to, I didn't want to; so, I carried on. Yet I knew it was harming me! I think I told myself that because I felt so truly horrific anyway, I may as well continue. Because for a short time I would have a drink and feel semi ok. I felt dreadful every day with the M.E. symptoms anyway, so I figured that it wouldn't make much difference if I was rough from drinking. But of course, it **did** make a difference! A huge difference.

There can be no getting around the fact that alcohol is a poison to our bodies. It can make us feel good, help us to relax, make us feel more confident, even make us forget our worries for a while... and all of this can lead to a dangerous cycle. I loved having a drink, and it was another lie that I told myself... that I may as well carry on as I felt so rubbish anyway. I told myself that I may even change for the worse if I gave up drinking. I worried I would become more boring, or that people would view me in a different manner. I thought that my life may not be as good without having a drink.

It's funny, as some people have said to me when they know the things that I have changed, that my life must be a bit duller. That I have 'given up' part of my life and I must not have as many pleasures to look forward to. This genuinely couldn't be further from the truth. The truth of it is, my life is far better now, better even than before I got ill.

Giving up alcohol was easier than I thought it would be. Again, I put this down to mindset. This was certainly one thing I could look at and see it as a poison. I decided I didn't want to have something so toxic in my body. It may sound harsh put like that, but it is what I tell myself to ensure that I'm looking after my body to the best of my ability. Of course, there are times where I have missed having a drink, but the benefits of not drinking far outweigh any cons.

I am not tee-total (although I was for the first six months of my recovery). There are times where I may choose now to have a drink or two... but it will be in circumstances where I know that the next day, I don't have anything to worry about and I can give my body enough R and R time.

I drink water. *Lots* of water! I also drink herbal teas. I drink a minimum of two litres of water a day and I find it easy to drink now. I love sparkling water and if I'm out, I like to have it in a gin glass with lots of added fruit! Maybe it's because I feel a little less obvious that I'm not drinking, who knows? But I know that drinking so much water benefits me in so many ways! I have recently started trying to add different things to boiled water, such as mint or ginger, the drinking it when it is cooled. This is great as it gives me different flavours and also has nutritional benefits for my body.

I do not eat sweet 'treats'. As I've explained, I was a total sugar addict. Most meals would be followed by a pudding, and I would have **lots** of sweet snacks during the day too. I had sugary drinks a lot too. So this was always going to be my biggest challenge! I used to tell myself that there was no way I could cut out my sugary treats. Yet I did. I won't lie... I'm ridiculously proud of myself for this, because it was difficult for me, and it is still one aspect I have to work on even now.

I will say that at the time of me giving it up, I was especially ill. I was at a point where I was needing help going to the toilet, I needed help with eating and all my energy was saved for the couple of hours I spent with my children where I chose to pretend that I wasn't as bad as I was. Even crying was really exhausting. Light, touch and sound hurt. Every inch of my body was painful. Looking back, it's so, so hard to remember that particular week because I can't believe how bad I was. It makes me sad knowing that I lived like that... and knowing that other people are still living and will continue to live like that (especially when there are still people who will tell sufferers that it's all in their head, or believe that it can't be as bad as all that).

I genuinely believe that because I was so very ill when I changed my diet so drastically, I didn't feel the withdrawal as much as I may have done if I *hadn't* been ill. I did have headaches and cravings of course, but they were nothing compared to the symptoms I was already experiencing. People without M.E. (thankfully) won't have that level of pain and illness to deal with if they decide to give up sugar/caffeine/alcohol/gluten... although it's important to be aware that there will probably be withdrawal symptoms and that you will have to get through them. It's hard and there's no point trying to deny it. To get through food 'addiction' and withdrawal takes a lot of mental strength and I would even go so far as to say, courage. It sounds daft in a way when you say it out loud... but anyone who has attempted to do it knows that the struggle is real. Not only do you have to get through the first couple of weeks, but you also then have to maintain it. But it **can** be done! I can pretty much guarantee that when you do it, you will start to feel better. You will start to look better. You will start to **be** better! It's **all** good!

I now make sure that if I'm going somewhere, I'm prepared with food. I was a bit embarrassed to do this at the start, as I thought people would think I was weird, but now I don't mind. It's far better to have food with me that I know I can eat, than to be caught out and end up either not eating or eating something which I will later wish I hadn't. I always try to make sure I have something healthy with me, and I also take herbal tea bags with me! I have been laughed at a couple of times, but I don't care. Usually, most people are good enough to understand that this is my new way of life. Plus, it takes pressure off people, as I know myself, there can be nothing worse than wondering what to serve people who eat 'differently'.

The main thing I have had to accept is that this isn't just a 'diet' or something which is short term. It hasn't been about losing weight. (Obviously I did lose weight which is completely understandable! I am happy I lost weight... not for vanity, but for my health! I know for a fact that I would have started to suffer with extra health conditions if my weight had continued to go up the way it was doing, as I put on roughly a stone each year I was ill.) It has been about me getting my life back. In fact, scratch that... it's been about making my life **better.** It's about managing my symptoms so that I can be confident in being symptom free. It's been about living my life not racked with pain, fatigue, brain fog and all the other nasty things which were making me so desperately miserable and having such an awful knock-on effect on my loved ones too. It has to be my way of life now **forever.**

I have accepted that while of course there will be times where I decide to have fish and chips, a piece of cake, or a glass of fizz, I won't make that part of my regular life again. I won't look at things like that and think it's a 'treat' because I have been able to change my mindset to such an extent that I genuinely don't see these foods as a treat anymore, quite the opposite in fact. That doesn't mean I won't be tempted! 40 years of eating whatever I wanted and eating a lot of what I would now call the wrong types of food, means that it can be difficult to not automatically want that slice of cake (especially if I am feeling emotional about something). But I am so determined to keep healthy, that I know that I will always make the right choice for me. I will 100% always choose wellness over illness. I will choose my complete happiness over five minutes of happiness eating something (which would usually be followed with guilt... although to be honest I've also worked on that too which is good! I don't believe we should feel guilty for eating certain foods, as guilt around food doesn't really serve us any purpose, other than making us feel worse... which usually leads to us eating more junk food in the end).

I'm happy that my new dietary changes will be with me for life. I accept that people may mock me, encourage me to eat differently, question why I refuse to eat certain foods and even call me boring for not eating or drinking what they do... but that's fine. I realise that if people do things like that, they have their own issues which they are projecting on to me. I choose to not let that sway or affect me in any way. My health and happiness will always come above everything else now. Plus, I don't ever want my kids fearing me dying anymore, so not eating particular foods is worth it! Every single time.

One thing I haven't yet talked about when discussing my diet changes, is the actual physical act of cooking. When you are ill, cooking can be something which is beyond your capabilities. Even something as seemingly simple as making a drink or a piece of toast can be too exhausting. Putting together a healthy meal which needs cooking from scratch can quite honestly be a pipe dream. I know myself that when I felt extra rotten, I would want to eat comfort/quick food, even if it was more likely to make me feel worse in the long run. This is where help is important. It can be hard to ask for help, and even if it is offered, it can be hard to accept. I would always urge anyone who is unwell to accept help... and if you are supporting someone who is ill, even in a small way, then helping them out with food preparation and/or cooking would be an amazing thing to do. There can never be anything detrimental in eating a healthy diet.

I also wanted to share some other things which can be important when thinking about what you eat... and that is *how* you eat. I'm a big believer in trying to practise mindful eating wherever possible. I do try to bring mindfulness into as many things as I can during my day, and eating is one place you certainly can do this. I know it's hard to sometimes sit and concentrate on your eating, but it can really help to make you feel a bit calmer in life when you do. Just taking the time to really appreciate what you are eating and being grateful for it can be quite beneficial for your mindset. When I am eating something nutritious, I really enjoy focusing on how much I am actually helping my body and being in more control of what is going on with my health, by eating such healthy foods. I try to make sure that wherever I can, I simply eat... without the distractions of watching anything, scrolling on my phone, or reading something. When I was very ill of course there was no way I could have even imagined being able to do both as sometimes I needed help simply eating, but now, I try to make sure I focus on eating my food.

I also try to chew my food up properly. This may sound daft, and even though it is grounded in science, we don't always do it. The more your chew your food up, the less the rest of your digestive system must do, so your insides don't have to spend as much energy digesting your food. It's all about conserving energy wherever you can. I think the guidelines are to chew your food 20 times before swallowing... which I appreciate can seem a lot. This is certainly where mindful eating helps too, as I know that when you are distracted by something other than eating, we often tend to chew less.

Making wise choices in your diet and thinking about how you eat, will undoubtably have a huge impact on your health. It can seem like a complete minefield out there when you look at what to eat and what not to eat, and there is so often conflicting information which can make it hard to know what to do. You may have eaten a certain way for so long that you may find it hard to imagine changing how you eat now. You may have been brought up believing that low fat foods and calorie counting are the way forward. You may not think that you have enough time to prepare fresh meals, and you may struggle with energy to even eat properly, never mind cook a meal from scratch. When you are willing to change your mindset about the foods you eat and the way you eat them, and you consequently change your diet for a truly healthy one, you will only ever feel benefits from it. It may feel hard at first, but it will **always** be worth it!

SUPPLEMENTS

Supplements have played a role in my recovery. While I fully advocate that we should try as much as possible to get most of our nutrients from the foods that we eat, I know that this is not aways feasible. Unfortunately, when you are ill, your body may not absorb nutrients in the same way as a fully healthy person. You may need different amounts of different things. With M.E. there is an issue with how our bodies create energy, so it is vital that various nutrients are in an abundant supply, as we can become even more unwell if we don't have them.

When I was not looking after myself to the best of my ability due to the diet I was consuming, I took a lot of supplements. I knew that I wasn't getting everything I needed from my diet if I'm honest, and so I felt fine with taking supplements. When I started being very health conscious, I did investigate whether I would still need to supplement, and I have decided to continue with certain ones.

Most of us have heard of vitamins and minerals and know that they play an essential part in our health... but not as many of us may be aware of what particular nutrients actually do and which ones we should be ensuring we have enough of. You may not know how much of something you need, or which foods give a good source of a nutrient. Labels will often shout out at us 'Rich in fibre', 'Good source of potassium', 'Naturally contains calcium'... but we may not know exactly how much of anything we are getting. Companies can be crafty with this of course and can advertise something in a way which makes it appear healthy, when actually it may only contain negligent amounts of any particular nutrient.

While I try to get all my good stuff from my food, I still choose to take some supplements too. I won't drop brand names in this area, as I know that this is endorsing something which I don't feel comfortable doing. As with most things, it is beneficial to get the best quality that you can afford... but of course that will vary drastically for everyone. So, I feel that for me to share what I use wouldn't be the right thing to do, as some people would be able to afford more than what I pay, and others would be able to afford less. It is good to do some research in this area and be aware that there are a lot of companies who may bump up prices, but not always offer great quality.

It is also important to speak to your doctor before starting any supplements. Some of them may interfere with medications and so it's vital that individual medical advice is sought to keep yourself safe.

The supplements I choose to take are Magnesium, CoEnzyme Q10, Iron, Calcium, Zinc, Probiotics, Prebiotics, a good quality multi nutrient powder, Collagen, Vitamins C and D, along with B vitamins.

I used to really dislike taking them. I found I had to almost force them down and they used to make me retch a bit! I much prefer to have a fully natural diet now and part of me objected to taking them. However, I realised that this was a mental block.

Maybe because I associated them with illness and my brain took a while to make the switch to seeing them as being part of my WELLness. When I initially wrote this section, it helped me to realise this, and I was actually able to change my mindset on it. I'm now completely fine about taking them and don't feel negatively affected by the physical act of taking them in any way.

As with everything, you must always remember that this is **your** journey, and what works for one person may not work for another. However, I feel that supplementing a diet when you know that you may not be getting everything you need, will work well for many people, and is something that should definitely be considered.

PHYSICAL ACTIVITY/EXERCISE/MOVEMENT

This is such a delicate subject to even bring up with anyone who has M.E. even when you are in recovery from it.

Prior to me becoming unwell, I had always loved to exercise and so having to give it up was a tough thing to deal with it. It wasn't quite as simple as giving it up either... it was adapting to a life where I sometimes couldn't even get out of bed. It almost sounds unbelievable when you realise how much M.E. can affect someone, especially when it is an illness with no one reason why someone may get it.

When I was having a 'good' day, I would be able to seem almost 'normal' for some amounts of time. I would be able to drive, walk with the kids and do some household chores. As time went on and I got worse, I needed a walking stick to walk even short distances. I remember one time when I had walked to the end of our estate to post a letter. It was not a long distance at all, maybe a five-minute walk there and back, but as I got to the post box, I knew that I wouldn't be able to make it back. I literally hobbled back, clinging onto my walking stick for dear life. I was sobbing every step of the way. I wasn't even worried about anyone seeing me like that because all I was able to concentrate on was the excruciating pain, and my desperation to make it home.

Days like that made me feel that it was impossible that I would ever get my strength back and be able to live a healthy life again.

M.E. has an appalling record when it comes to how it has been treated. From having horrific 'nicknames' such as 'yuppie flu', 'lazy disease' and 'tired disease'... to completely misguided advice on how to deal with it. Research on this illness has been massively underfunded and it is so very frustrating to see how it is still so low on medical agendas. Of course, since the Covid pandemic and the onset of Long Covid, there may well be more funds given to research M.E. since so many of the symptoms are similar. (Indeed, since I started writing this book I have taken part in the biggest study there has been to date, 'DeCode Me', so I am hopeful that more help may be on the way in the future.)

In the past, Graded Exercise Therapy (G.E.T.) was recommended for people with M.E. as a way of getting them up and about, even if they were in a bad way. The problem with this illness is that sometimes even the slightest thing can set you back so much. When I used to exercise when I was well, if I pushed my body a bit harder than usual, I would feel some pain. I may be stiff for a couple of days and maybe I would struggle to raise my arms up or walk properly. I'm sure that most of us will have experienced that. In fact, I used to quite like that feeling. I felt like I had worked hard and while it may take a bit of time to recover, I believed that I was doing my body good in working it and getting fitter.

If you have ever experienced that and can now remember that feeling... I can tell you that it is absolutely **nothing** like the feeling you get when you have M.E. It is genuinely so hard to relate anything to how bad you feel, even if you try.

When you have pushed your body, then you can often expect to feel some aches and pains. You know your body needs a bit of recovery time and you know that your body is working hard... but it's all good because it's all working properly. With M.E. your body **isn't** working properly. You don't have to push your body hard to make it hurt. It can be the smallest thing which causes what is known as Post Exertional Malaise (P.E.M.) It could be going for a walk, driving a car, talking to someone, making a cup of coffee, reading a book, writing in a diary, walking up the stairs, or even picking something up off the floor! Sound dramatic and like it's not possible? Yet that's exactly how it is! It doesn't just cause stiffness and aches which you know will be gone in a couple of days, and a bath or relax won't just help magic it away. It's horrendous pain; it's utter exhaustion; it's being unable to get out of bed; it's wondering when, or even if, you will ever get back to your baseline again. It's debilitating and it's so upsetting. It does not surprise me in any way that people who have M.E. will quite often end up having other issues like depression, anxiety and panic attacks on top of their illness... because it can affect you mentally so much.

The thought of exercise/physical activity when you feel so unwell is ridiculous for a lot of people. However, I do feel that it's an important thing to talk about here as it was part of my own recovery. As always, this isn't about me simply giving advise as such to people with M.E. but sharing what worked for me and discussing some of the benefits I feel that even people without M.E. could take from my words.

I missed exercising so much. It had always been a big part of my life and I felt that I was losing yet another part of me when being able to do it was taken from me. Exercise was a way I kept my body healthy... and my mind too. I loved going for a run whenever I was worrying about things as it gave me a chance to clear my mind. There were days when I was feeling rubbish and my husband would tell me to get out for a run, as he knew it helped calm and de-stress me so much. It was also a good way for me to socialise, as I had friends I would go running or to gym classes with.

I am a big believer that exercising is good for the body and the mind... and there's plenty of scientific research out there to back up my own beliefs. Even if you don't especially like the thought of traditional exercise, getting outside and going for a walk is a huge thing that you can do for yourself. It doesn't have to be about beasting yourself at the gym either, there are so many things now that are sometimes gentler, such as yoga or tai chi, which have a great effect on both body and mind. Dancing is so much fun that you may not even view it as a form of exercise. And of course, anyone with a dog knows that their daily dog walk certainly constitutes exercise.

When I became unwell, I totally had to change my way of thinking. The 'old me' was still telling me that **I should** be able to do things. I was sadly very unkind to myself. I would crawl up the stairs sometimes and call myself pathetic. I would question what had gone so wrong with me that not only could I no longer run, but some days I couldn't even get myself to the toilet. I was mentally and verbally berating myself so much... and it was horrible. I wouldn't *dream* of talking to anyone else the way I spoke to myself, and when I look back, I am filled with sadness for the cruel way I treated myself. I would dream about being well enough to exercise again, while often not actually believing it would ever be possible for me.

I remember the M.E. specialist I saw telling me that it was important to 'do more on my bad days and less on my good days'. Well, I totally misinterpreted that, until I fully understood what she meant. I would push myself hard on my bad days, thinking that was the right thing to do - less on good days and more on bad days. But you must be **so** careful with what that means. It doesn't mean go for a run on your bad days and go for a shorter run on your good days!! It is where I believe mindset plays a huge part again. On your good days, it's very tempting to try and do lots of things, because you may feel guilty about things you haven't been able to do. You figure that you may as well make the most of the energy you have while you have it. This may mean that you end up doing activities which you know (if you're truly honest with yourself) will end up causing more suffering in the long run. You may try to do household chores, or go for a walk, or meet up with friends for that little bit longer or watch a film which you know may trigger you, or even make yourself a meal. This is only going to cause you to crash and then the bad days get worse, and more common.

Then on your bad days you may try to push yourself by thinking that you would normally go for a 100-metre walk, but I'll do a 200-metre walk - so you are doing more on your bad days. But it isn't about that at all.

This is a really hard thing to get right and its good to pace yourself. It's about making sure you do the bare minimum on your bad days, so that you don't end up feeling worse in yourself. Your bare minimum may be making it to the toilet on your own... and if that's the case, then so be it. This will be an **achievement** and should be treated as such. Celebrating even the smallest win is an amazing, and I believe necessary, thing to do.

On your good days, rather than thinking about doing all the housework that you haven't been able to do, settle for doing one job instead, then you aren't exhausting yourself.

It's tough. Really tough. Especially if you are also worried about other people judging you (which is yet another reason why working on your mindset is of such importance). I had so many people ask me if I was 'all better' or 'cured' now when they saw me doing something outside the house... without being aware in any way that me getting out of the house may be the only thing I was doing that day, or even that week.

Exercise was something I wanted to deal with when I started recovering, as I was so desperate to start doing it again. I would try and push myself to go for walks. I knew I couldn't run so I didn't attempt that. I found myself getting more and more despondent the harder it became to walk, and there was a time when it made me want to stop even trying. It felt pointless. I half thought that if I couldn't run or go for a long walk like I used to, then there was no point in even trying. Plus, I also felt selfish. I felt that wanting to exercise for myself was going to take me away from things I could be doing with other people, especially my children. I felt that even though I loved to be outside, even if only for a short time, it wasn't fair for me to do that if it then meant that I had to go to bed early and didn't get to do an activity with the kids. This is why I truly know that mindset is so important in this because you have to see that looking after yourself is a real priority, even if at times it means that you feel that you are letting other people down.

When I made my decision to fully commit to myself and my recovery, I had to change my idea of 'exercise'. I had to accept that from now on, for however long it may take, I had to have different goals. I had to learn to be ok, in fact to be more than ok, with achieving small steps. I had to be my own cheerleader and applaud myself when I did things which I would have once taken for granted. I needed to be happy for the seemingly simple things like getting up and down the stairs, as some days this would be a huge thing for me. I needed to take things slowly.

It was hard. I so wanted to get my strength back and to be able to do more and more.

I scaled back in the things I did, but I did things with more *purpose*. Rather than push myself to do things which I felt I **should** be able to do, I started to do smaller things which felt good, and didn't make me constantly worry about the payback. I stopped putting myself under pressure, and that was a big one.

I started doing a little bit of 'bed yoga' (and no... that is not a euphemism for something else). I started celebrating things more, for example, walking up and down the stairs, so that I felt boosted. I may not have been running a 5k first thing in the morning anymore, but I would applaud myself for managing a short dog walk. I really think that when you start celebrating the small wins, it helps your mindset so much. One of the worst things you can do is to compare yourself to your 'old' self when you are ill... so I stopped doing that, and it made a huge difference.

I would incorporate small things into my day which helped me feel like I was making progress. And I *did* start to make progress. While I would certainly advise caution in any type of exercise 'regime' when you are ill, and I think medical advice is always a good idea, I found that with all the other changes I was making, my strength and energy were starting to make a comeback. This was where I had to be careful as I had learnt from experience that if I pushed myself now, I could end up setting myself back a lot.

So, I remained patient. I could see the physical changes (as could the rest of my family) and I held myself back from trying to run before I could walk. I slowly stopped using my walking stick as much. I started being able to walk that little bit further. I was able to bend down and reach up without too much pain, and I could feel myself becoming more flexible again.

After a few months of solid improvements with no major relapses, I decided I wanted to reach for the stars. I decided I wanted to try and run again. Obviously, this was a huge thing for me, and I discussed it with James, as we were both worried about whether it was the right thing to do. I decided to opt for the NHS Couch to 5k programme, which aims to have you running for 30 minutes continuously after approximately nine weeks of working up to it. It's set out so that you start off slowly and build your way up. However, even though you start off slowly, from where I had been, even the start was tough. It was walking for a few minutes, then running for 60 seconds, and repeating that.

Honestly, the first time I heard it, my mean girl crept in and whispered "60 seconds? How pathetic are you? You used to run 10k in 45 minutes! Just bloody run if you want to run!" (She sounds a bit like a moody/nasty teenager if you can imagine that!). Then the M.E. protective voice jumped in with "What the *hell* are you thinking?! You can **not** run!! You will relapse and undo all the good work you have done! Go back to bed right *now*!" (She has a very matriarchal, don't mess with me voice!)

I kindly, but firmly, shushed them both. I knew that the mean girl was just being mean and serving no purpose, while the M.E. voice was coming from a place of fear and meant well but was keeping me back a bit. I told myself that I would, of course, listen to my body, but it felt like the right thing to give this a go.

The first time I ran again was so strange. As soon as I stared, I didn't want to stop! It felt amazing! I felt like Forrest Gump (in a good way) when he just runs and keeps on running! I was so exhilarated... nothing could stop me... this was meant to be... and then all of a sudden, I knew that I had had enough. I checked... and I was about 50 seconds in! GO ME!!! And I do not say that being sarcastic in any way! Genuinely, I was delighted! I knew that I had wanted to run for so long, and I had done it! 50 seconds was a mammoth achievement and the start of this new journey back into running!

I followed the programme while listening hard to my body. I always had the recommended rest day in between each run, and some days I needed more than one. Some days I repeated the runs I had already done, as I knew I wasn't ready to go up to the next level yet, and I was ok with that!

Eventually the day came where I ran 5k! I cried!! Big, fat, chest heaving sobs. I couldn't believe it. My whole family were so delighted. The kids made me congratulations cards and were cheering me on when I got back from it. It felt wonderful. Unlike in the past, before I became unwell, I didn't automatically think 'what next?' I was happy with where I had got to... but I knew that it was enough. My body (at that time) could not have handled anymore, and I wasn't willing to risk it by pushing myself any further. This was quite difficult for me, as I have realised that I was so used to pushing myself that it seemed unnatural to not be looking for another challenge. I didn't want to try and beat my time or go for a 10k next. (Don't get me wrong, I would like to work up to a 10k at some point, but I'm in no rush to do that as I'm quite happy with where I am right now. I have complete faith that I **will** keep on getting stronger and healthier of course, but I won't ever push my body the way I used to.)

I love that I can do more physically now and even when I have days, or even weeks where I don't do any set exercise, I don't mind as I don't feel the same pressure I used to. I think in the past, exercise for me was more about trying to keep slim and fit than it was to do with my actual health. I needed to be fit for my job, and I like to be slim, but I never really thought about all the health connotations like I do now. I want to keep my body moving, but for all the right reasons... to keep me **healthy.**

While this chapter has been one of the most difficult ones to write about as I'm well aware that for so many people with M.E. exercise may only ever be a pipe dream, I hope that this chapter can provide people with hope that with faith, determination and making important changes in your life, it **is** possible to get a good level of energy back so that you can exercise in the future.

MEDICATION

I will start this chapter by stating that I am ridiculously grateful for modern medicine. I believe in most vaccinations; I am all for life saving treatments and operations; and if I've been in an accident, you can be damn sure I want a trained doctor looking after me. I reach for painkillers when I feel I really need to and will give my children Calpol if they need it. I would never say no to any medication that I thought would help save my life or make pain more bearable. I have been brought up knowing how lucky I am to live in a country where we have access to free treatment and medicine.

When I became unwell, I went to the doctors fully expecting that I would be offered something which would 'cure' me. What a shock I was in for!

Initially I was offered antibiotics for my chest infection. This first lot did nothing, nor did the second lot. The steroids I was then prescribed put me in hospital because I had such a bad reaction to them. However, I was still happy to trust the doctors and expected they would come up with another solution which would fix everything. (Side note... you will never hear me bash any of the doctors I saw as I am in the lucky position that they were all good!)

However, a 'quick fix' wasn't to be. One huge issue with M.E. is that there isn't (currently) a medical cure. There isn't a magic pill which suddenly makes everything ok. There isn't even a course of pills which will make everything ok in a week, a month, or even a year. There isn't something you can take which may make you worse for a while but will then eventually hopefully destroy whatever is harming you and make you better.

All that can be offered are things which may, or may not, help to ease some of the symptoms. The problem with that of course, is that a lot of medications aren't designed to be taken long term... and if they are, they often have to be taken in conjunction with other medications to balance out what one drug is doing to you. When you have been diagnosed with a condition where you don't have any idea as to how long it will take you to recover... or even if you will **ever** recover, then that can start you off on a slippery slope.

I want to reiterate here before I go any further, that I wholeheartedly stand by people taking medication when they need it. 100%. There is nothing worse than when someone advises you to simply meditate and then you won't need any more drugs (and hey, I'm a big believer in meditation as you will find out... but I am not going to advise it over taking medication if you truly need it).

The problem I had personally, was that I didn't want to be on medication for the long term. I had no issue taking something short term, as I wanted to believe that it would help me. But what happens when what you are taking doesn't have any affect? Or even worse... makes you feel worse?!

When I first got ill, the fatigue, flu-like symptoms and brain fog were my worst issues. The pain didn't start straight away. Unfortunately, it did arrive before too long though. Bone-crushing pain. It was so hard to explain to anyone as it wasn't really like anything I had experienced before. I hadn't injured myself; I hadn't overworked a muscle; I had no idea what was going on. Everything hurt. I used to try to focus on something which didn't hurt on my bad days to try and find something positive. Some days it was my hair and fingernails which I used to think about because they were the only things which didn't hurt!

I went back to the doctors again about all of this new pain. Along with the fact that even though I was absolutely exhausted to the point where movement was wiping me out some days, most nights I couldn't sleep! Even when I did manage to sleep, I would wake up feeling like I hadn't, as I never felt properly refreshed.

The doctor prescribed some tablets which would hopefully help me sleep and alleviate some of the pain. The first doses didn't make any difference, so I had to up the dosage quickly. After a while, I found that I *was* falling to sleep... but then the mornings after were horrific! They had been grim before, but now I was like a true zombie! I couldn't function at all and felt like I was a danger to myself!

It was hard at that point, because I knew my body needed sleep, but I had two children to look after. I couldn't afford to be taking medication which made me feel unsafe. Caught between a rock and a hard place, I had to try and work out what was best for me.

The pain got gradually worse. I ended up needing stronger painkillers... then stronger again as my body got used to what I was taking. Different types of painkillers were tried and then I was advised that if one worked out, I would need an extra drug as it would affect my stomach long term. It was so upsetting and frustrating.

At one point my doctor tried me on tablets which had had some success for patients with fibromyalgia. He warned me, as usual, that it may or may not work and I would have to see how I got on. He also said that it was an anti-depressant and so that I may experience some mood differences.
Well... that was a really scary time.

I remember only about three days into taking them waking up one night while my husband was working away. I checked my phone to see the time and saw I had a few messages on my phone. I decided that I didn't want to open them later, as I didn't have the energy to speak to anyone (even via text). I then decided that I was an awful friend, and the fact that I couldn't do things like I used to, and that some friends had disappeared since I became unwell, must mean that I didn't deserve any friends. This then swiftly moved to what an awful wife I must be and how poor James must be getting fed up with me and would probably be better off without being married to me. Then onto what a rubbish mum I was; how I was letting my children down and how they deserved someone better.

It was a truly dark time. I **knew** that this wasn't me, I knew this wasn't my 'normal'. A little voice was telling me that none of this was true. But a louder voice was shushing that little voice and I felt like I couldn't fight back.

I lay awake for the rest of the night with these awful thoughts tearing through my mind. I didn't even have the energy to cry.

The next morning my mum (who was staying with me while James was away as I couldn't be on my own anymore) commented on my state, as did my kids. I somehow took the children to school and two of my friends told me straightaway that I looked drastically different. I realised that the medication I was on wasn't for me.

I phoned the doctor and thankfully got an appointment that same day. When I walked in, even the doctor could sense I was different. He explained again that because the drug was an antidepressant, it could make me feel worse before it made me feel better. However, and this is the big one, I was **not** depressed! My heart goes out to anyone suffering with clinical depression, because that small glimpse into a very dark hole made me seriously scared and I cannot imagine how that must feel on a longer-term basis.

I discussed it with the doctor, and we agreed I shouldn't continue with the medication. If I had been dealing with depression, I would certainly have been willing to try to get through the initial difficult time with it; but I wasn't prepared to feel worse mentally than I did without having those drugs in my system, especially given the fact that there was no guarantee that they would even work for the pain.

My point in sharing this particular story, is that it can be really hard to know what the right thing to do is, especially when you are ill. It's important to be able to have a good doctor who will listen to you, take the time to get to know you (which can be rare given how stretched doctors now unfortunately are), and accept that what they recommend may not be the best thing for *you* as an *individual*. I know it can be hard if you have been brought up to put your trust in doctors - but please be ok with putting yourself first and if someone isn't listening properly, don't be afraid to go to someone else. I am so grateful that I was strong enough to be able to listen to myself and know that those drugs weren't right for me. Of course, for someone else they may be the **best** thing they can take and may change their life, but it truly is an individual journey!

When I was in the police, I had seen many people who had ended up becoming addicted to painkillers and other prescription medications. I found it scary how someone could end up this way after an accident, an injury, or an illness, such as M.E. I knew that it could affect people who were not 'drug users' in the typical sense, but had got to a point in their lives where drugs/medication were the only thing helping them get through the day, and now they couldn't stop taking them. This was then having a detrimental effect on the rest of their life.
I knew I didn't want this for me.

I was taking more and more tablets. I realised that they weren't really doing that much for me. They sometimes would for a while... but then I would need an increased dose to get a result. I was being advised that the next option was medications I really didn't want to take as I knew how addictive they could be. I couldn't see a way out of this cycle, as I knew that all the medications weren't curing anything - they were simply an attempt to *mask* some of the symptoms I was suffering with.

I decided I didn't want to continue like this. I knew that there was only me who could make the changes and do anything about this.

Obviously, when you are on prescribed medication it is not as simple as just stopping taking it. I knew that I would have to be careful with how I did this (and again, time for me to add that if you are looking to do this yourself, **please** seek professional advice as stopping taking drugs can have a huge impact on you and needs to be taken very seriously).

When I started my proper recovery journey, I was on quite a bit of medication, which I hated. I wished I could just stop them, but my pain and fatigue prevented this. However, as I made all the changes to my diet, changes to my lifestyle, followed all of the advice from the M.E. course which I was doing, stuck to my supplements, partook in the alternative therapies... I found myself feeling better. This encouraged me to try to reduce my medication and to my delight, I found that this seemed ok. I continued to gradually reduce it... and am very happy that I can now say I am fully medication free and have been since about six months into my recovery! This feels amazing to me! Knowing that I am not having to put unwanted and unnatural drugs into my system helps me feel better mentally and physically. In fact, I have noticed that I deal with other things much better now and without the need to reach for painkillers, such as period pains. Of course, I fully accept that there will probably be times when I do need medication again, and I'm honestly fine with that. I'm just delighted that I no longer have to contemplate the possibility of spending a lifetime on medication which isn't even having a brilliant effect on me anyway.

Medication can be essential for so many of us for so many different reasons, and it can often be a first port of call nowadays as we have become so used to dealing with our ailments in this way. So, while I will never criticise taking prescribed or over the counter remedies, it is important to realise that there are other ways to heal. I am a huge believer in a holistic approach to healing of any kind. That does not necessarily mean *only* using alternative methods. It means using a **variety** of different methods and finding what works for you. It isn't saying meditation over medication, as there can be room for both in a recovery journey. One thing you must accept with this illness though is that there will never be a quick fix! No doctor will be able to prescribe something which will get you better in a week, a month, or even a year. That is a difficult concept to grasp, I know! When you accept your illness and surrender to the fact that your healing is on you, then you will certainly be able to begin your own healing journey. When I say surrender, I do **not** mean that you give up. The one thing you should *never* do is give up. You **can** recover from M.E. There are so many people out there who have recovered already, are recovering today, and will continue to recover in the future. When you start to look to yourself to heal, then your true journey of recovery will start!

ALTERNATIVE THERAPIES

If you are anything like I **used** to be, you may cringe a little bit when you hear the term 'alternative' or 'holistic' therapies and think that they are a little bit 'woo woo'. You may tell yourself that 'these kinds of things' aren't really 'your kind of thing'. You may be thinking that you prefer to 'follow the science' and that modern medicine will be a much better alternative than the 'alternatives'. If this type of thinking applies to you, I would still encourage you to read this chapter rather than simply dismiss it... as I really feel that I have been able to make huge beneficial changes to my life due to becoming open to alternative therapies.

It wasn't that I was completely dismissive of alternative/holistic treatments prior to being ill. I didn't really know that much about them. Even though my limited experience of them pre-M.E. had actually worked out well, I didn't really believe that they would be all that effective in helping me. I guess that when anything health wise went wrong at any point, I just opted for the more modern methods of reaching for some sort of medication out of habit.

What do I mean when I talk about alternative treatments? There are so many, and the amazing thing is that they have been around for thousands of years! The fact that so many of them are still in use certainly says a lot about their effectiveness. While I will always be grateful for modern medicine and appreciate that it can, and does, save lives, I do feel that if more people were aware of holistic therapies and would be willing to consider and use them more, there would be less illness (which would have the added benefit of being less of a strain on our health care system). In the same way that when you take care of yourself by controlling your diet and so can help to prevent (and even cure) certain illnesses, I believe that looking after yourself with the use of alternative treatments can really help you stay much healthier.

I have been fortunate enough to try a lot of alternative treatments, but certainly haven't tried all of them. There is energy healing (such as reiki), reflexology, herbal remedies, acupuncture, aromatherapy, Emotional Freedom Technique (EFT, also referred to as 'tapping'), light therapy, massage, homeopathy, hypnotherapy, Chinese medicine, crystals, electro-magnetic therapies, K-laser treatment, infra-red sauna, as well as practices such as meditation, mindfulness, and yoga.

Some of these are now more mainstream than others and in fact, you may not even have thought about some of them as being 'alternative' until you really think about it. Massage, for example, is something which people consider a real luxury, but don't always link the health benefits from it, other than knowing you feel more relaxed after. You may find that you would be more willing to try one thing over another because it feels more acceptable as it is in the mainstream, but I would urge you to not write something off because you think it sounds a bit weird.

My first experience (pre illness) of reiki was a bit of a strange one. I was in the police at the time and had gone to a police rehabilitation centre as I was having a bad time and had been especially ill (with hindsight, I can now see that this time of my life was certainly a pre-cursor to me getting M.E. and I was trying desperately hard to ignore the horrible symptoms my body was sending me. I was experiencing excruciating stomach pain which did not go for weeks, even though the doctors could not find anything wrong (other than an ovarian cyst which was removed but did not stop the pain)).

While I was in the police rehabilitation centre, I was told that I would have certain treatments. I was really excited as I had seen massage on the list and so off I went, expecting to have a nice relaxing massage. I was *not* impressed when I got to the room to be told I was having a reiki session! A 'Whaty?' I asked! I hadn't even heard of reiki. When I was told about what it was… someone putting their hands over me and sorting my energy out (this was my take on it anyway) I was even less impressed! I wanted a massage, not some 'hippy' (sorry… it's what I used to think) hovering her hands over me. I'm pretty sure I was sulking inside, even though I put up the pretence of being grateful for it. I did not expect that reiki would do a thing for me and decided that it was going to be a complete waste of time.

I lay on the bed while the therapist explained what would happen. She told me that I may experience heat, or coldness, or feel a little bit odd. She said I may even fall asleep, at which I scoffed, as I hardly ever slept at things which other people seemed to doze off to. She got started, and I lay there grumbling inside my mind. Mourning the fact that I wasn't getting a lovely massage. Feeling nothing.

Then, suddenly, she moved to near my stomach. My whole body felt like it had been doused in cold water. I opened my eyes to see what the hell was going on. To see the lady standing over me with her hands hovering over me and a look of peaceful concentration on her face. No water in sight! As she continued, I got a strange feeling and I wanted to cry. At this point I was starting to wonder what was going on… but decided I should probably just keep quiet and let it continue.

As the session continued, I began to feel calmer - much calmer than I had done for a long time. The feeling stayed, but not in a negative way. When she finished, she asked me how I felt, and I explained what had happened. She said that she had felt an energy surge at the same time I had and that she sensed I was worrying about something important to me. I hadn't told anyone at the time, but I was worried that I wouldn't be able to have children due to a few issues I had experienced for a few years. I felt more at peace about this than I had done for a long time and decided that I should try to stop dwelling on it as much.

I did do some research on reiki after this session and was really intrigued by it. It had felt so powerful, even though I went into it with a very cynical, and even quite negative mindset. I did wonder how it would be if I went in with a much more positive mindset. However, for some reason, I never tried it again until my illness.

The other experience I had was with acupuncture. I was involved in a police car crash and suffered with severe whiplash. My right shoulder was in a bad way and my colleague suggested his wife may be able to help as she was currently training to do acupuncture. He sold it to me as he said I would be doing her a favour as she needed guinea pigs for case studies. The people pleaser in me fell for that one and I agreed to give it a go. It was not what I expected as she put the pins in my ear. I had assumed that she would put them in my shoulder, as I did not really know anything about it other than I was about to be a human pin cushion. Again, it really did help me much more than I would have ever expected it to. I had a few sessions and it helped with the pain so much!

So, with two positive experiences under my belt, you would think that I would be more than happy to consider alternative therapies as soon as I got ill. But I wasn't. I was still stuck in my conditioned mind of thinking that modern medicine would have all the answers. It was horrible when I realised that it didn't. That there was no official treatment. That there was no cure. That this could be a lifelong condition where there may not be a cure found in my own lifetime, especially given that when I first got diagnosed, research into M.E. was ridiculously underfunded and in no way a priority.

Thankfully, I was fortunate enough to have a wonderful friend, Vanessa, who had just become the manager at a place near me called The Sanctuary of Healing (Langho, Blackburn). When I got ill, she suggested I come over for a consultation and some therapy.

Here began my healing journey aided by alternative treatments. I have found that the more I investigated the treatments and different ways of healing, the more interesting it became... and the less I was willing to rely on modern medicine. After I had decided that I wanted to try and reduce, and hopefully remove, medication in my life, I knew I had to have something to help alleviate my symptoms. I am so grateful that I have been able to find ways to do that.

I know some people would use the phrase that 'alternative treatments aren't for everyone'... but I disagree. The beauty of them is that they can be for everyone, as long as you are willing to give them a chance. You may find that one thing suits you better than something else. One thing may have little impact, whereas something else may be literally life changing. There is some trial and error with it, which puts some people off. But I found that even with modern medicine in M.E. it is often a case of trial and error anyway. The medications I had been trialling were having more of a negative impact on my body, as drugs sometimes can! I didn't like the thought that I was inadvertently harming my body in an attempt to heal it! With alternative treatments, there is little risk of harming your body (although obviously it is always advisable to seek medical advice, and to go to professional therapists when trying anything new).

I would struggle to recommend one treatment over another if anybody asked me, as I really feel that it is a personal choice. A bit like one drug will work for one person, it may not work for another (although, as I have said I do feel that the benefits of trying out holistic treatments are that you aren't likely to make yourself ill trying different ones.

One of the biggest things which needs to be taken into consideration when looking into this route is unfortunately the cost. I find it really upsetting that for people with M.E. (and other illnesses) that they can be prescribed drugs by doctors, but it is very unusual for them to be guided towards alternative treatments, and even more rare that they will get any for free or at a reduced cost. I won't lie... alternative treatments have cost me a lot of money over my illness and throughout my recovery. They will also continue to cost me money as I 100% believe in their effectiveness and think that if I was to stop them then my health may not be as great as it is now. I have seen first-hand that when I have stopped treatments for whatever reason, I feel worse. They are a huge part of my self-care.

When I first started going to The Sanctuary, I had an initial consultation with the head therapist there, who was able to recommend what would work well for me. The Sanctuary has a lot of experience with M.E. patients and so it felt good to be somewhere where my symptoms were taken seriously, and I felt like I was getting advice from someone who not only cared, but who knew what they were dealing with properly.

I started my alternative healing journey with Crystal Therapy (TheraGem). Theragem uses precious and semi-precious gemstones with low-level light technology to help restore your body to health. It works by focusing the healing wavelengths of the gemstones so that your natural healing system is activated, which will then balance and regenerate injured cells and tissues. When directed at the skin (I had them at my temples and spleen), the light, colour and energy produced positively affects the human energy system.

I also coupled this with Electro Magnetic Therapy. This is a safe and effective method which can restore the body's electrical balance and stimulate healing. It essentially recharges our cells (a bit like recharging a battery) by restoring their positive and negative charges. The body's ability to self-heal and self-regulate by restoring cellular communication is optimised.

If I'm honest, I didn't expect it to do much... and at the start I didn't really notice much difference. I did end up wondering whether it was working after a few sessions... and then I had to have a break from having them due to childcare issues. Boy, did I notice a difference then! I think sometimes you don't realise what an effect something is having on you, until you stop. I realised quickly how much of a benefit those treatments were having on me, and so did my family. They gave me so much more energy, and a lot less pain. I knew that they were really helping me, and they have been a great help for me in being able to manage my symptoms. If I knew I needed an extra boost of energy for any reason, this was the best way to achieve that.

However, I did have to accept that while I was having these sessions, I was unable to do anything else. I initially found it very difficult to lie there and do nothing. Even though I was physically unable to do much, my mind would go into overdrive. One of the worst things I dealt with emotionally was guilt. I would feel guilty for the cost of the treatment, guilty that I wasn't doing something else for somebody else, guilty for being unwell even! I would sometimes use the time to be on my phone. I got caught one day though and was firmly (but kindly) told that this time was precious, protected time where I should fully focus on my healing. I wasn't helping myself by finding other things to do and I certainly got a lot more from the sessions when I gave myself up to relaxing, and *healing*, properly.

If these treatments are not available to you, then there are alternatives which can be investigated. You can purchase crystals from a variety of sources, and they do not have to be expensive at all. A quick internet search will give you lots of information about which crystals may benefit you personally and advise you on how to best use them. I have several crystals at home which I use, and I wear crystals on pieces of jewellery too. So this particular alternative treatment does not need to cost a lot of money or take up a lot of time.

After enjoying success with the magnetic therapies, I decided to wear magnetic jewellery. I researched about it after I had my treatment and decided that I wanted to have more ongoing benefits from magnets, so chose to wear magnetic health bracelets. Again, these can be picked up from various shops or internet stores and needn't cost a lot of money (I would recommend a little bit of research to ensure that you are getting a quality product.) I wasn't initially sure how effective these were, until I had a couple of days of not wearing them. I noticed a difference in my pain and fatigue levels. I bought mine from a company online called Bioflow. Although it wasn't overly cheap, I wear it every single day so feel it was worth it for me.

Reflexology is another treatment I have tried a few times. This is a type of massage which involves applying different amounts of pressure to the feet (it can also be used on your hands and your ears). It is based on the theory that these particular body parts are connected to certain organs and body systems. It is believed that by applying pressure to these parts in a particular way, a range of health benefits can be achieved. It was traditionally used in ancient China, where it was believed that everybody has vital energy, which they called 'qi' (pronounced 'chee') flowing through their body. When a person is stressed, their qi becomes blocked, and this causes an imbalance which can then lead to illness. The aim of reflexology is to keep qi flowing through the body and so keep it balanced and free from disease.

I had reflexology on my feet and my therapist explained about how different parts of my feet are connected to different parts of my body. When certain parts of my feet were massaged, it affected the energy in that correlating organ or body part. Luckily, I have no issues with my feet being touched so I really enjoyed the treatment.

It was very relaxing to have it done and I had a couple of times where I could certainly feel energy flowing differently around my body, which was somewhat surreal. I felt quite tired after the therapies initially, but my energy increased for some time after the treatment. I found that I slept much better after reflexology too, which is always a complete blessing.

Most people have heard about massage, and it is probably one treatment which a lot of us would be the most willing to try. In fact, even if you don't ever go for an actual massage, most people are likely to use massage in their everyday life without even thinking about it. When we have a headache, or we bang ourselves, or have soreness somewhere, we will automatically massage the sore area! It's easy to see then that massage has great health benefits and it's wonderful that we can even apply this treatment to ourselves at any time!

Massage is a general term for pressing, rubbing, and manipulating your skin, muscles, tendons and ligaments. It can range from a light stroke to the application of deep pressure on an area. There are many different types of massages, and so it is likely that everyone can find one which will work best for them. A deep tissue massage would not have worked for me when I was very unwell, as my body was far too sensitive, and so it would have been far too painful.

Massages have several benefits. They stimulate your nervous system; invigorate your muscles, organs, and glands; move blood and lymph fluid and gets cells to produce and release chemicals and hormones. They can reduce muscle pain and soreness. Massage relieves stress and anxiety and can help you sleep better. They can improve your immune function and even increase your flexibility. Plus, they feel amazing! It's easy to see why they have become so popular, and many people (whether unwell or not) may be more likely to treat themselves to a massage than many other types of alternative therapy.

Massages are available in a lot more places now, as they have drifted into the beauty industry as well as the wellness arena. You are likely to be able to find a practitioner in a local beauty salon, which is great for a lot of people. I do feel it is important to try to find someone who has had experience working with people who have M.E. or a different assortment of illnesses and so can be understanding of the different needs wherever possible. I know from when I was very ill, sometimes even the lightest touch would be physically painful and so there were times when massage would not have helped me. But when I was able to have them, I always felt great after.

Even if you cannot have massages with a practitioner, this is certainly something that you could look at doing yourself or getting a trusted friend or family member to help you with. While a professional massage will obviously always produce the best results, it can still be effective having a gentle home massage. The human touch is very therapeutic (if you can handle being touched of course) and so can produce a lot of health benefits for you. Even just the physical act of relaxing into a massage will help you feel that little bit better. It is also worth noting that local colleges, beauty salons, or friends/acquaintances may offer treatments at a heavily discounted price (or even free) while they are training students, so this is something which is worth looking into.

I would say that the treatment which has had one of the biggest impacts on me in my recovery journey has been Reiki/energy healing. So much so, that I went and trained to do it myself, so that I could have more control over my own healing and life.

Reiki is a traditional Japanese form of energy healing, which promotes relaxation, reduces stress, reduces anxiety, and improves the flow and balance of your body's own energy to support healing.

It is administered by practitioners 'laying on hands' (some practitioners will hover their hands above you while some will gently touch you) over certain parts of your body. Reiki is based on the concept that an unseen 'life force energy' flows through us. If this energy is low, then we are more likely to get sick or become stressed. Reiki can help people become more energetically balanced – physically, mentally and spiritually. It complements other types of medical and therapeutic treatments and can increase the efficacy of other types of healing.

Reiki has so many benefits. It can stimulate your body's immune system and promote natural self-healing. It can relieve pain and tension. It will support the well-being of people receiving other medical treatments. It can foster tissue and bone healing after injuries or surgeries. It can bring on a meditative state and so is wonderful for helping people to relax.

Since I had already had a reiki session and had felt great results, I felt much more hopeful going into it when I was unwell with M.E. Because reiki is non-invasive and I always felt so relaxed after, I knew that it was doing me a lot of good. I would feel physically and mentally so much better after a session. My energy was boosted, and I just felt better and able to deal with things in a much calmer way. It felt brilliant knowing that I was doing my body good and not harming it any way. Reiki is simply working with your own energy and encouraging your own body to heal naturally, and I absolutely loved that idea.

Emotional Freedom Technique (EFT) is something I have learned about which has been **very** helpful too. It is also called 'tapping' and it is so ridiculously simple and easy to learn, that literally anyone and everyone can do it! It is something I have also taught my children to do as I believe it is so powerful. Quite simply, tapping involves tapping on certain (acupressure) parts of your body while saying or thinking certain affirmations/statements/words. You can do this yourself and use your own words to make it personal for you and your own situation, or you can follow a guided tapping system. I have a tapping app on my phone so that I always have quick and easy access to a number of different ones. You can literally find something for pretty much any given situation or emotion you may be feeling. There is a set pattern to it, whereby you follow a technique of tapping on different areas (the side of your hand, eyebrow, side of your eye, under your eye, under your nose, under your mouth, under your arm and the top of your head). You learn how to say certain statements which initially acknowledge a particular issue (usually negative), then accept it, before moving on to something positive which can help to make you feel better. This helps to send calming signals to your brain and can be effective.

I appreciate sounds so simple that you may struggle to believe that it can work. Especially given that you can literally do it at any time, anywhere and it can take as little as two to three minutes each time! However, it has scientifically proven benefits and it is even being used for people suffering from PTSD. I would most definitely encourage you to have a look into this as it can help with both emotional and physical symptoms of M.E. A quick search on the internet will pull up more information and even guided lessons, so you should be able to find something helpful to you personally.

I would urge everyone to consider alternative/complementary/holistic treatments no matter what their level of health is, but *especially* if you do have any health problems. Of course, I would never say don't take medications as they may be necessary for so many people... but it is always worth looking into other options as an additional way of helping you recover.

I was delighted to totally go medication free after a few months of committing to my recovery stage. I am not naïve enough to think that I will never have a use for medication in the future, as I have no idea what is around the corner for me. However, I truly do believe that my new lifestyle which combines the many helpful things I do will help to keep me well. I choose to heal my body in the most natural ways I possibly can and have been very fortunate to have had such good results. I would never say that any of these therapies will **cure** you of M.E. (or any other illness) ... because if it did then the doctors would (hopefully) be prescribing it. I would like to hope that sooner, rather than later, more doctors will be open to recommending these types of therapies as complementary along with any medication they prescribe. It would be especially amazing if they were available free of charge or at a reduced rate to people with illnesses who would benefit from them.

PACING

Prior to being ill, I had only really heard of pacing in the context of pacing myself during a run. I took it to mean not setting off too fast and keeping a steady pace so that I didn't burn out and be unable to finish a race/run. I never for a minute dreamed that I would one day have to live my whole day to day life by pacing myself.

When you start researching about M.E. or speak to anyone with any experience of it, one of the first things you hear about is pacing. You get told to 'learn to pace'. I didn't really understand it at first, as when you first get ill you have no idea what is going on. You are waking up day after day hoping that today is the day that you will feel ok. You push yourself a bit as you want to believe that you will be able to cope. Then you feel utter despair when you realise that things haven't suddenly got better. In fact, quite often, they may have even got worse. It is soul destroying.

I was referred to a chronic fatigue specialist clinic after my diagnosis, and one of the things I was advised to do was to pace. I genuinely didn't know how I could do this at that time. It may seem silly to say that... but when you have gone from a life of always being on the go, to a life where some days you needed help being fed or being taken to the bathroom, it can be hard to learn how to adjust to it.

Pacing is so simple... and yet so very difficult. Many people who are diagnosed with M.E. have come from backgrounds where they have been super busy. The idea of just slowing down a bit may be alien, never mind slowing down to an extent where you must prioritise your activities and possibly accepting that if you are going to have a shower in the morning, you may have to spend the rest of the day in bed. Sounds extreme, doesn't it? Yet, unfortunately, for so many people with M.E. it becomes a reality.

It can be difficult to explain what it is like having M.E. and how much it affects your energy. People may assume that they know what it feels like to be so tired or can even try to relate it to when they have had the flu or something similar... but it cannot be related like that in any way. Of course, you may understand what some of the symptoms feel like... but the longevity and extremeness of it all is so tough to get your head around. Since Covid, there have been a lot more people who may have more of an idea though, as people are unfortunately suffering with Long Covid.

One of the best theories I heard and one which I used to explain it to my husband who found it helpful for his own understanding (and it also helped us at home when he would tell me to 'save a spoon') is The Spoon Theory. It was coined by a lady called Christine Miserandino in 2003, who used it to express how it felt to have lupus. It is used to describe the amount of physical or mental energy a person who is ill has available for daily tasks and activities.

While sitting with a friend and trying to explain how she felt living with her illness, Christine handed her friend 12 spoons. Each spoon represented a unit of energy. She asked her friend to think about the typical activities you would do each day and relate each task to a spoon. Every time a task was mentioned, a spoon was taken away. So, for example, showering may be one spoon, as could getting dressed. Making breakfast, doing your hair, watching TV, speaking to someone, sorting the kids...all these were spoons which were being taken away. All these activities could be ones which have occurred before you had even left the house. Some tasks may be worth more than one spoon. For example, driving may take three spoons, going out for lunch may be three, working may be five, housework could be four, reading or studying may be three etc. It's easy using this analogy to see how quickly your precious 'spoons', or energy, can be used up. If you only have 12 spoons in one full day, it can be difficult when you are trying to work out how to use them.

I think this is an effective way to show people how it can feel and how hard it is to live life when you have such little energy left for things, simply because you have used your energy up getting out of bed, getting ready and feeding yourself. You may have used more than half of your daily available energy in under an hour!

It isn't like when you are generally unwell, and you just feel a bit low on energy. You can't think that you will just have a good night's sleep, or a quick power nap, or even some fresh air and you will suddenly feel energised again. Recovery from doing **anything** can be difficult. You may be at a point were leaving the house to go out for lunch with a friend can mean it takes a week in bed to recover. Life becomes hard when you must prioritise in such an extreme way. It isn't simply about saying no every now and then so that you can catch up on rest - it can be about saying no all the time to seeing people or doing certain things, because otherwise you won't have enough energy to cook and eat food.

It can sadly be hard for other people to understand as well because they may see you out and about and think you look fine, without realising that you are using all your 'spoons' to do one thing. They may not realise that they have seen you once seemingly ok, but that you have then had to spend the rest of the week in agony and had to cancel everything else you were planning on doing. So again, it can really affect people when they are told that they 'don't look ill'. It can lead to isolation as people either stop inviting you out or judge you when you do manage to make it out or can't understand why you are cancelling seeing them (as they don't realise that you simply don't have enough energy to do the simple things if you risk going out).

I used to want to try and save my 'spoons' to do a school run and pick up the kids. It was important to me (pre-committing to my recovery journey) that my children saw me doing that... even though it meant that I would be in so much pain and a lot of days it would be the only physical thing I could do. I would have to fully rest to be able to do it, and I had to prioritise things to be able to do it. Of course, I was very aware that people would see me doing this and possibly assume that I wasn't too bad, because I was making it outside. At some point, you *do* have to accept that people will always think what they want to, and you must be ok with letting it go. Easier said than done I know, but worrying about what other people are thinking or saying about you is a complete waste of a spoon (and when you think of it like that, it really isn't worth a precious spoon).

In all honesty, I didn't pace properly until I decided to fully commit to my recovery. It sounds daft as you would think that you would straightaway do something which you are told will help... but we don't always do the sensible thing. A bit like diet, and mindset work, and all the other things which we know can help us... it can be a lot to suddenly make changes, even if they are ones which will benefit us. We are creatures of habit and quite often will stay stuck in our comfort zone, even if the reality of it is that the comfort zone is partly responsible for making or keeping us ill and/or unhappy. It's a tough thing to come to terms with and admit to... but when you really think about it truthfully, you will see lots of examples of this all around you. I can honestly say that I was doing it myself, and I'm glad that I now have the courage to be able to admit to it... and that I have also had the strength to change it.

Pacing properly really does mean making a commitment to prioritising things in your life. Unfortunately, there is no way of knowing whether your day will be a 'good' day or a 'bad' day... but you do have to do what is best for you each day to try to make it as good as you can. This will inevitably mean that there are things which you cannot do. There will be things you have to cancel and people you have to say no to. I appreciate that all of this sounds disheartening, and in truth, it is! It's so hard when you really want to do things, but your body says no. I always think of the David Walliams and Matt Lucas sketch when he says 'computer says noooooooo'. I used to try to inject some humour into being unable to do something by joking 'Body says noooooo'. It's not funny of course, but then a decade in the police did leave me with a somewhat warped sense of humour, so I think I will blame that!

Pacing involves working out what is **really** important to you and ensuring (or attempting to) that you save enough energy for those things. Some days, it will be all you can do to get yourself out of bed and eat. For severe cases, even that may be too much sadly. Some days, you may feel pretty good, and your symptoms may be totally manageable. Those are the days I had to be extra careful. If I didn't pace on these days, I would be lulled into a false sense of security and would end up setting myself back.

I think it's important when you are ill to try and have as much support as possible, and so explaining about pacing is vital for those supporting you. There still isn't enough awareness around M.E. and with it often being an invisible illness, people can really struggle to comprehend it. Even I struggled to get my head round it, so I always tried to tell myself to be patient with people who appeared unsympathetic and couldn't seem to empathise. I found a good website which I would share with people about M.E. (**actionforme.org.uk/get-information/what-is-me/symptoms**) in the hopes that they would read it and understand a little better.

Your family and friends need to be able to understand how important pacing is for your recovery/management of the illness. I needed to explain to my children in a way that they could understand why mummy sometimes couldn't do the things they wanted me to do. It was hard...especially when I had spent so long trying to put a brave face on so that they wouldn't realise how unwell I was. When Jack had confessed that he thought I must be dying, I initially wanted to push myself even more so that he would think that I was ok... but I soon realised that this could only ever be counter-productive as it would end up making me more ill. When I committed to changing my whole lifestyle for a minimum of six months, all the family knew what was going on and were thankfully very supportive of me.

Pacing for me meant accepting help... a lot more than what I used to be comfortable with. It meant accepting that I couldn't do certain things like picking the kids up, no matter how much I wanted to. It meant resting **properly.** This may sound like a simple thing to do, and you may think that everyone can rest, and rest effectively... but I disagree. We have become used to being so busy and always having something occupying us, that actually switching off and resting is not really the norm any more. When you think of resting, you may think about lying in bed or sitting on the couch...but how often will you also be doing something else at the same time? Do you watch TV, read a book, listen to music, talk on the phone, chat to someone with you, scroll on social media, check your phone, do some emails, check the news, play a game? All these things may **seem** restful, in that you may tell yourself that they are helping you relax and unwind. You may think that they are helping you switch off from a busy day or helping to entertain you and so this is beneficial for you while you are resting (and if you aren't ill, then this can certainly be true). But the truth of it is that by doing any (or all) of these things, you are not actually *properly* resting. You are keeping your mind engaged and so you are not switching off properly. In fact, you may be activating certain parts of your brain or nervous system so that you are actually more active in some ways than you are when you are doing a physical activity. If you are doing any of those activities, your brain is unable to switch off and your ANS (autonomic nervous system) is being triggered. This can have a detrimental effect on someone who needs genuine rest.

When I was unwell, I did not rest properly for the first couple of years. I didn't realise that I wasn't resting, as I assumed that by me lying in bed, lying on the couch, or having a bath, then I was resting adequately. I simply did not think about the fact that a lot of the time I would be keeping myself busy by doing other things (especially by being on my phone so much). Unless I was sleeping, I hated 'resting'. I realise now that one of my main issues was guilt. I felt so terribly guilty for resting. I guess boredom played a big part too as it can get very boring lying or sitting there doing nothing... especially when you aren't used to it and when your brain/mind isn't trained in a way which makes this rest seem acceptable.

I felt that at least if I was doing 'something' I couldn't be as ill as I felt (if that makes sense). I clearly struggled to really accept my illness for a long time when I look back at how things were.

Part of my pacing meant cutting out or cutting down on some of these things (I will go into more detail about this in another chapter). It meant that my rest periods were **real** rest periods. Time where I didn't distract myself with some sort of technological entertainment. I started to meditate (more of that later too) and I learned to be ok with not doing certain activities. It was hard. Really hard. I was wired, as so many of us are (and especially those who may end up with M.E.), to be on the go most of the time. I already knew I had taken such a step backwards in life because I couldn't do everything I wanted and initially this felt like an even further step back. But it was what I needed. The body cannot heal if it is working without proper rest... and by keeping my mind switched on, I wasn't allowing myself the rest I so desperately needed.

I worked out what I did want to achieve each day and I made myself a list on a whiteboard, hung up in my room so I could see it. However, I made sure that my mindset was such that I wouldn't beat myself up if I didn't accomplish everything on my list. As time went on, I deleted a couple of the things which I had thought were important, but then came to realise that they weren't. Likewise, I was able to add a couple of things which gave me even more time for myself when I realised what a big impact on my own healing I was having by being truly kind to myself.

Pacing meant me getting comfortable with saying **no** more. It didn't always feel good, but I knew that in the long run, I would be so thankful to myself for doing less. There is only ever so much we can do in any given day, and yet we try so hard to be wonder woman/man, often to the detriment of our own health.

Even in my recovered state, I still choose to pace myself daily. I refuse to slip back into my old ways (even though sometimes I can feel the pull towards being that people pleaser and the person who struggles to say no). I do not want to ever be ill again in the way I have been with M.E., and I know that it is *on me* to keep myself well to the best of my ability. I now have the mindset that by me saying **yes** to something which I don't *truly* want to do means that I will be saying **no** to *my own health and wellbeing.* I accept that other people may feel 'let down' by me saying no to them – but I also know that this is actually *their* issue and not mine!

Life is too short and too important to do things which make you miserable – and pacing myself helps me to ensure that I am making the best of this one life which I have been blessed with.

RESTING

Getting proper rest is so important for everyone, but *especially* for those of us who become unwell. The thing about 'resting' is that we all have quite different ideas about what rest actually entails. Some people will keep quite active, even when they are supposedly resting... because that is what helps them feel relaxed! There is a difference though between *resting* and *relaxing*. My husband loves to watch TV and it helps him feel relaxed - it helps him to rest his body, because he isn't doing anything physically active. However, for me, watching TV can never be truly restful, because it is triggering my ANS and keeping my brain working (it's also doing the same for James, but thankfully he doesn't have to contend with M.E. so can cope with different levels of things).

If you think (the same way I used to think) that resting simply means lying or sitting down, then you are only a little bit right. Resting doesn't just mean slowing your body down....it means slowing your mind down too! It means switching off from things which you may enjoy... but which don't allow you to properly rest. It means not reading, writing, watching TV, playing on games, scrolling through social media, talking on the phone or in person. Honestly, that can be quite extreme!

When I was ill, I didn't rest properly for a **long** time, and I'm absolutely convinced that I stayed unwell for a longer time period because of this (as well as all the other detrimental things I was doing). I would rest my body of course... mainly because I had no choice a lot of the time. My body just wouldn't physically move sometimes.

I struggled to rest my mind as much as I could have done. Of course, there were times I physically couldn't even read, write, use my phone etc because of my overwhelming symptoms, but I found that if I was able to do something along these lines even for a short time, I would do.

What I needed to do was properly rest. As in no phone, no TV, no book, no writing pad, no computer – just resting in a chair or a bed, with my body inactive. Lots of these rest periods are needed when you are ill, and they actually need to be taken seriously. As in a DO NOT DISTURB sign going up!! As well as DO NOT ALLOW DISTRACTIONS too!!

I won't lie... it's **hard**! Really, really hard! It should be simple, right?! It should be *so* easy to properly rest! After all, surely we all want to feel rested and recharged and then able to take on the day? My guess is that many people may now struggle to properly rest, whether they have good or bad health.

I think one part of the problem is that we think that resting is boring. God forbid we get bored nowadays! We live in a society where we have so much on offer, and we have entertainment at the switch of a button. We don't have to wait or look around for long for something to entertain us. Even on long journeys we have things to entertain us and long gone are the days of only playing 'I spy' or the lorry game in the car with the kids... they can simply watch a film or be on some sort of electronic device! We can have constant sound with the radio on or can be on the phone to someone while travelling. We literally *never* have to be alone with our thoughts... unless we choose to! Of course, that doesn't mean we aren't sometimes lonely, but my point is that we never have to be without something to occupy our minds!

When you think about it, life has become quite overwhelming! How many of us wake up in the morning and the first thing we do is reach for our phone? We check our social media accounts, read the news headlines, and even check our work emails... all before we have even got up to go to the toilet sometimes. We are switching our minds on and tuning into the outside world, without giving ourselves chance to look inwards and focus on ourselves for even five minutes!

Throughout the day we are bombarded with information in so many different forms. From getting on with our regular daily activities, working, looking after a family, sorting a home, exercising, seeing people, and getting out and about... it can seem never ending! Think about how much noise and visual interactions come your way every day! Your phone, computer, TV, the radio, music, the internet, social media... it doesn't end even when you think it has! In the middle of the night, you may wake up and reach for your phone. Even if it's just to check the time, chances are that if you see some sort of notification on your phone, you may end up being drawn into checking what's going on in the outside world, which will of course distract you from going back to sleep.

It's no wonder that even people without M.E. or other serious illnesses are so often exhausted! We rarely seem to fully switch off! We aren't giving our brains and minds the rest they so desperately need. Our energy is being spent on constantly keeping going. Even if you think you are resting, you may not truly be.

I felt it was necessary to write about this separately, because I think it's of such importance that we realise how necessary *real* rest is... and acknowledge how likely it is that we may be kidding ourselves a bit as to how much true rest we get.

When you are ill, it is vital that you allow yourself real rest. Of course, I agree that you can't always 'rest yourself better' with serious illnesses... but if you can guarantee that you are getting proper rest, you stand a much better chance of helping your body recover at a faster rate than if you are 'resting' while watching TV, reading or playing on your phone (all things I used to do by the way).

This may mean setting aside time to rest, which is what I ended up having to do. It may sound daft, but I struggled with 'real' rest because it felt like I was failing. It was one thing being bed bound one day (or lots of days) ... but to choose to not do *anything* felt extreme. Of course, this is where mindset came into play. I reminded myself that I wasn't, as I feared, doing *nothing*... I was, in fact**, recovering**. I was doing what I needed to do to try to effectively *heal* my body. I was being completely selfless actually - as the better I got, the more I would be able to join in life again and give to other people when my energy allowed. This last thought really helped me. As a mum I had to overcome a lot of extra mum guilt through my illness and so the thought of being better for my kids certainly benefitted me.

Meditation helped me get through all of this and is one way you can help yourself when resting (I will discuss this in a later chapter). I guess it helped me feel that there was more 'purpose' to what I was doing and having purpose is a big thing for me. It also helped me get rid of that feeling of 'boredom', as well as that horrible worry about whether I was 'lazy' (I'm not by the way, and I'm confident you aren't either).

Resting may or may not bring sleep. I won't say I'm a 'bad' sleeper and always have been -as I try to avoid negative affirmations wherever I can! But let's just say sleep hasn't always been my forte! Even when I was a child/teenager, I really struggled getting to sleep. It would always take me ages to get to sleep, even when I was exhausted, and so 'power naps' never worked for me. I used to try them when I had my children and they usually ended up backfiring! I would finally manage to drift off after an hour of trying, to be woken up within five minutes by a child... which ended up making me feel worse.

I am a light sleeper too, so often had disturbed sleep. And of course, once I had kids, that threw decent sleep straight out the window. Even now, when they are eleven and nine, and generally sleep well through the night, I'm still so in tune with them that I will often wake with a start, and within a minute will hear the sound of one of them getting out of bed for one reason or another. Sleep hasn't always been easy for me. I wish I had discovered the benefits of meditation years ago and decided to commit to it, as that would have made any rest periods I had much more successful.

It's hard to believe, but even when you have M.E. and feel constantly fatigued, sleep can be really difficult. I would often lie down thinking sleep was inevitable, for pain to then keep me awake, or another symptom to flare up and stop me from falling to sleep. I used to find it very frustrating trying to get to sleep, which ended up having a negative impact on how I was feeling, which of course made everything worse. I believe that if I had thought more about 'resting' being a **healing activity** in its own right, I may have felt better throughout this journey.

Now, I ensure that I make time to rest every day...whether I feel like I need to or not. This is for much shorter times now that I am doing so well, but it's very important that I still do it. I know I need to properly switch off and rest properly. This means putting my phone away, switching off any electronic devices, moving away from anything which may distract me, and simply 'being'.

We seem to have forgotten that we are human '*beings*'....and feel more like human '*doings*' now, as so many of us find it so hard to simply **be**. Instead, we are always *doing* something!

I would highly encourage everyone to take some time out, and 'do' nothing other than be content to just 'be'. (If you struggle with the idea of that, always remember that you are never **really** doing *nothing*! You are always breathing, digesting, repairing cells, pumping blood and lots of other things which you can't see and usually take for granted! Think about how much more energy you can give to all those things that your body does... and how much your body will thank you for it when you give it a chance... by resting.) Ironically, I found that when I learnt how to rest properly, I needed less time lying around!!

SLEEP

Ahhhh sleep. That blissful end to the day when you fall into bed, tired after a busy day, close your eyes and gently drift off for a full eight hours; before waking naturally, feeling refreshed and ready to start the day with renewed energy. Unless, of course, you have M.E. in which case none of that is true! Before I got ill, I used to *love* my bed! During my illness, I grew to pretty much hate it because I felt so miserable in it. I hated how even though I was exhausted, I really struggled to get to sleep. Even when I did manage to get to sleep, I would very often be woken up due to the pain I was in. It was just horrific.

For quite a long time, I did rely on medication to help me sleep. I 100% needed that medication at that time, as I desperately needed sleep and so I would never say that any medication is unnecessary. It most certainly has its place in this illness! If you aren't getting proper sleep, then you will never heal properly. If you can't get decent sleep, then it may be worth speaking to your doctor to see if they can help you.

The issue I had was that as my body became used to the medication, I ended up needing higher doses all the time. The side-effects weren't great for me, but cutting back on the drugs meant that I wasn't getting proper sleep. It is an awful situation to be in.

I decided that I needed to follow a good pattern with regards to my sleep and be fairly strict with it. The thing is, I knew what I *could* and *should* be doing with regards to getting a good sleep, but I didn't always do it. Sleep is such a sensitive subject as, even without illness, so many people struggle to sleep well for a variety of reasons. I think that so many of us tell ourselves (affirm) that we are 'bad' sleepers, without realising that just us saying this can have a detrimental effect on our sleep! If you are telling yourself that you don't sleep well, then it will become a self-fulfilling prophecy. For years I was sabotaging my own sleep by not doing the things which would help me have a good sleep!

Sleep is a bit like diet and exercise. We have all heard lots of advice about it and have a good idea of what we should be doing, but we often choose not to do the things which will help us. We may try something new a few times, find it doesn't work straightaway and so claim that it doesn't work for us; and then give up. It's amazing how many people drink caffeine during the day, even late into the evening and still expect to get a good night's sleep, even though scientific research can prove that caffeine stops us getting a good sleep. I've heard people say that caffeine doesn't affect them either way with their sleep. These are always the people who then complain about not sleeping well and I wonder if they committed to cutting out caffeine for a significant length of time, how things would change! So many of us may have bad habits surrounding sleep and it can be hard to change them. But if you genuinely want to make a difference to your sleep, then you **must** be prepared to *change*.

For me, sleep was now more essential than it ever had been, and so I knew that this was going to have to be part of my commitment to myself. The same six-month period I was giving myself to make all the changes was the same amount of time I was giving to try to optimise my sleep. It was hard at first, as I realised that I had picked up so many unhelpful habits over the years. Even now, it's one area of my life where I can slip up. In fact, now I'm thinking about it, it's often harder for me to commit to a good sleep routine than it is to control what I eat!! It can be easy to pick up my phone too close to bedtime, even though I know that I am likely to suffer when I do that!

I researched about how to get a good night's sleep and made sure I did as many helpful things as possible.

I made sure that I got outside every day and tried my best to get out as early as I could. Our bodies have a natural time-keeping clock which is called as the circadian rhythm. It affects you by telling your brain and body when to go to sleep, as well as helping you to stay awake. Natural daylight can really help keep this system working effectively, and if you can get out in the morning, it really optimises your ability to sleep well!

I had already cut down on my screen time (which will be discussed more in another chapter), but I wanted to make sure I was doing the best I could whenever I did use them. I started to wear blue-light glasses. Blue light is emitted from electronic devices and can trick your brain into thinking it is still daytime! When we look at our evening habits and realise how many of us may be using screens late into the night, often even using them in bed, it's no wonder that our sleeping may not be so great! I had to stop using my phone in bed, which was hard if I'm honest, as I was in the habit of using it a lot at night-time! I would even use my phone in the middle of the night if I woke up for any reason. It was a good distraction, but it was stopping me from getting a good night's sleep! I stopped watching TV at night and started putting my phone away (although I did use it for night-time meditations which I will come to). I have a blue-light filter on my phone too which helps to reduce the blue light.

I cut caffeine out! (I do now have very small amounts occasionally.) Caffeine is known for its ability to enhance energy, focus and even sports performance; so it's no wonder that so many of us love it! It certainly can be a hard habit to kick! We may find ourselves craving that boost it gives us, and so end up having a lot more than we should be having if we are hoping to get a good sleep. Caffeine stimulates your nervous system and so can prevent your body from naturally relaxing. It can stay in your blood system for six to eight hours after consumption!! This truly shows that if you are drinking it in the late afternoon, or even the evening, it is very likely to be keeping you awake for longer!

I went to bed and got up at a similar time each day/night. I wanted to be in a good sleep pattern and did not want to spend hours in bed where I wasn't sleeping.

I knew it was beneficial to see my bed as the place where I slept, rather than as the place I spent hours **not** sleeping. It was hard, because some days it was difficult to even physically get out of bed. Bed was a place of safety in a lot of ways. I wasn't risking falling or hurting myself due to weakness if I stayed in bed. I knew that was an unhealthy relationship to have with my bed, but unfortunately when you become so ill that you can barely move at times, you don't always have much choice. I tried my best though and thankfully after some time, this got easier to do.

I supplemented with magnesium which actively helps to promote good sleep. I also had magnesium baths during the week and found a magnesium body lotion which I used in the evening as both can help improve relaxation and enhance the quality of sleep.

I also used natural remedies such as lavender on my pillow, as this has a calming effect on the body.

Cutting out alcohol was part of my new diet regime anyway, but when I was researching sleep, I also realised that this would help with my sleep too. Alcohol consumption is known to lead to disrupted sleep patterns. It alters night-time melatonin production. Melatonin is an important sleep hormone which tells your brain when it is time to rest and go to bed. No longer drinking alcohol certainly helped me to sleep better.

I didn't eat late in the evening. I used to be a habitual snacker. Previously I would eat my evening meal and then continue snacking until late on! This was having such a detrimental effect on my sleeping! I was filling myself with foods which would keep me awake, since they were often laden with sugar! Plus, when I was eating chocolate (I was a complete chocoholic) I was adding extra caffeine into the mix! I changed to eating my evening meal and leaving it at that for the rest of the night, which definitely helped!

I made sure that my bedroom was a welcoming space. I'm not a fan of untidiness anyway, but I made sure that we kept our room as tidy as possible. I never wanted to be lying in bed and thinking that the room needed sorting out. It may seem like a little thing, but it's important to optimise your sleeping area so that you are giving yourself the best chance to get a good sleep. We made sure our room was dark, and at a good temperature (not too hot, tempting as this was as I was very often cold), with a window open as often as we could for some fresh air. I have a lovely house plant by my bed, which is known for releasing more oxygen at night-time. We got bedside lamps so that we didn't need the main lights on when we got into bed. We also bought the best bed that we could afford. We knew that being as comfortable as possible would give me the best chance to get a decent sleep. A good quality mattress helped as it reduced the general pain I was in. I hadn't realised until we swapped beds how much of an effect the bed itself was having!

Every single night, I committed to a night-time relaxation practice. I would make sure that I spent time quieting my mind. I used to find that as soon as I got into bed, no matter how exhausted I was, my mind would suddenly switch on, and often go into overdrive. I found that what worked best for me was to do a guided sleep meditation. James bought me a really fabulous gift one day which has had a big impact on my sleep. It is an eye mask which has built in headphones in! You can connect it to your phone via Bluetooth, so you don't even have to have your phone next to you once you are set up! I would pick my meditation, pop my eye mask on, and amazingly, drift off to sleep! Some nights it would of course take longer than others, and even now some nights it can still be a struggle. But generally, I have found something which really does work. I like to listen to different meditations, including deep healing sleep meditations and also positive affirmations while you sleep ones.

If I wake up in the night (even when I reduce my water intake, I still end up getting up in the night to go to the toilet) and I can't get back to sleep quickly, I will simply put on another sleep meditation. I also don't get caught in the trap of negative self-talk through the night. I used to tell myself that I was rubbish at getting to, or getting back to, sleep. I would then start to dwell on the thought that I wasn't going back to sleep. I would calculate the sleep I had already had and the number of hours I had left to sleep. I would start to clock watch and get panicky about how many hours I had left in bed until I had to get up. I worried about the effect not being asleep was having on my body. The more I worried, the more awake I became! It was a vicious cycle and I realised that I was creating more problems for myself. I wasn't in control of my own mind as I was letting my thoughts rule me. I got caught on the hamster wheel of one negative thought after another coming in, and this was just about the lack of sleep, never mind all the hundreds of other thoughts which could come into my head at night.

Mastering my mindset has been one of the best things ever, and my sleep has improved because of it.

When I was really ill, I would often have to sleep during the day. If I'm honest, I absolutely hated doing it. It never felt right for me, and I would wake up feeling extra groggy. I never quite managed the art of the power nap.

Even though I didn't like day-time naps, for a good while they were necessary for me. I simply couldn't get through the day without at least one. I did worry that it would be having a detrimental effect on my night-time sleeping, but I knew that I needed the sleep to heal, so figured I didn't have a choice.

As my recovery went on, I was able to reduce, and finally stop my daytime naps, which I'm really pleased about! Ironically, I can sometimes do a guided meditation during the day and find myself naturally drifting off. The wonderful thing is that I wake after a very short time, and I do feel refreshed! This only happens if I am lay down to mediate and so I only do this if I am feeling extra tired, as I don't want to associate general meditations with sleep.

There really are so many things which we can do to help ourselves get the best possible sleep. It may be a matter of trial and error... but it 100% is about commitment. Like anything, if you decide to try something out and only give it a couple of attempts, it is unlikely to really work. Just like someone who decides to eat healthily and then expects to lose a stone within a couple of days, it simply won't happen. It means dedicating some proper time to yourself. It means making changes which may feel strange at first. You may have to break years' worth of habits. You may have to give up things you enjoy. You have to stop telling yourself that you are a bad sleeper and that things which work for so many other people simply won't work for you. As Henry Ford famously said, 'Whether you tell yourself you can, or you tell yourself you can't, you are right'. Start affirming that you are a good sleeper and put some work into making new habits which will help you become one. The benefits are endless! Our bodies heal when we are asleep, so for anyone who is ill, good sleep is absolutely essential!

M.E. COURSES

When you are told that you have an illness with no medical cure and no official treatment, it's fair to say that you can feel very discouraged. Most of us now end up on good old 'Dr Google' for most ailments, and I was no different! It wasn't long before I saw advertisements for different M.E/CFS/Fibromyalgia courses. I had no idea what was involved with them so naturally investigated them and found myself in a bit of a maze.

It's so hard when you feel lost and often helpless. With no official guidance from doctors about alternative treatments or courses, it can be difficult to know what to do or where to turn.

There are a variety of different courses on offer designed to help you manage your illness and help you recover. They can cost a lot of money and with no guarantee that they will even work, that can be a big risk to take.

I was incredibly lucky that when I started going to The Sanctuary, they were running in-house M.E. courses, coupled with treatments. At first, I was reluctant to go as I didn't believe I did have M.E. I was in denial for quite a while and at the point of being offered the course, hadn't had my official diagnosis. I was living in hope that one day I would just wake up and it would have all magically vanished and I could carry on with my life the way it had been. Thankfully, I was persuaded to give it a go and I'm so glad I did.

As I sat in the first session, the wonderful man leading it, Malcolm, described how certain people may be more prone to getting ill with M.E. I sat listening and silently crying. The tears just wouldn't stop flowing as he pretty much described **me**. It was like he had a tick list, and I was thinking "That's me, and that's me, and that's me" with everything he described.

The rest of the group were so supportive and when he had finished talking all turned to me to check on me. I wailed that I had felt like a fraud and didn't even think I should be taking up a space there... but now I could see that unfortunately, I did. It was a big realisation, and one I clearly needed.

The course lasted for six weeks, once a week for two hours. You had a treatment included each week alongside the course itself, so it was wonderful. (I had Theragem/electromagnetic therapy.)

It helped me learn more about what M.E. was and taught me some good techniques for helping me deal with my symptoms. It made me feel better in knowing that it wasn't (as some people think) all 'in my head' and that I wasn't going crazy, or depressed (although obviously that can certainly be a consequence of getting ill with M.E. due to how much it changes your life.

It was also good to be around other people who were in a similar situation to me. Whilst I found it very distressing to see how many people did suffer, and the length

of time lots of people had dealt with it for, it felt reassuring to know I wasn't on my own. M.E. can make you feel lonely and isolated, so it was good to have a group of people who understood me when I said certain things.
I loved this course and know it did me a lot of good. However, being completely truthful, I didn't get the best out of it. Purely because I didn't implement all the changes recommended on the course. It's so hard to put your finger on why we quite often don't do things even when we **know** they will benefit us... but the truth is that so many of us don't do the best by ourselves! Maybe it felt like too much hard work at the time. If I'm honest, just living and getting by was exhausting, and so the thought of making changes was sometimes too overwhelming.

It took me a lot of self-development to realise things about myself which were holding me back. I know now that we *do* hold ourselves back, and keep ourselves trapped in our comfort zone, even if that comfort zone is harming, rather than helping us. I needed to be fully ready to do *whatever* it took to recover. Of course, I know that some people may think that is daft and that you should be prepared to do whatever it takes to get better from the start... but I know that it takes hard work and determination to do that and we aren't always ready instantly.

We all know that we should be eating healthy food... but do we always do that? We know we should be exercising regularly... and yet many of us don't! We know that alcohol, cigarettes, and drugs are toxic to our bodies... and yet many of us choose to take them. We know that we should be doing so many things which could benefit our lives... and yet we stay stuck in a cycle which stops us choosing to them! If you read any of this book and **know** that you 'should' be doing something differently, please know that you aren't alone. You need to be fully ready to give it all you've got. For me, that took me having that horrific week where all I could see was that I was heading in a downwards spiral and I knew that if I didn't act there and then, I may never head back up.

I had looked at several different M.E. courses and eventually decided to do one called 'ANS Rewire' by Dan Nueffler (ANS is your autonomic nervous system). This course genuinely did help me change my own life... but please re-read that sentence. This course genuinely did **help *me* change my own life.**

You can do *all* the courses in the world... but if you don't do the work, you won't get the results! It can never be enough to sign up to a course, watch some videos, read some books, attend some sessions; and that be all you do. You must **do** the things which are recommended. If you don't take action and make the changes, then you may as well just be throwing your money away.

So, while Dan's Course helped me massively, and I have no qualms in recommending it, please know that his course, or any other similar course, will only work if you are willing to put the work in.

I had been on Dan's CFS Unravelled Facebook site and thought he made a lot of sense. I started the ANS Rewire course by initially getting his book to see what I thought. Honestly, some of it completely bamboozled and overwhelmed me! However, there was enough in there to encourage me to give it a go.

Dan is a former M.E. sufferer himself and has managed to recover from it. He shared his story and what he did to help himself recover... and has since gone on to help other people change their own lives.

The course entailed being sent a different video every day for about two months. Some of the videos were quite short, some a bit longer, but no more than about 45 minutes. Some days I could watch one and take it all in. There were times where I would watch one video and had to rewatch it a couple of times for it to sink in. Other days I could only watch half of one before fatigue took over. The videos were great though, as you could simply watch them at your own pace. Initially I wondered why they weren't just sent all in one go... but it soon made complete sense as I think I may have been tempted to try and rush through them, rather than taking the time to really digest everything in them.

Dan is a scientist and so backs up a lot of what he says with science, but not in an overwhelming way in the videos. I committed to doing whatever he advised on the course... and I stuck to it. The course encourages you to look at **everything** in your life, so you are truly encompassing a holistic way of dealing with everything.

At the end of the course, I was quite sad that it was the last video. I had come to enjoy them so much and I had truly garnered so much valuable information from them. I had made all important changes, which I could already see were helping to change my life! I finally felt in **control** of my recovery... and that felt wonderful!

It was while I was doing the course, that I realised that all the changes that I was making, and the commitment I was making to myself, needed to be lifelong. The course helped me come to terms with that. It helped to give me the faith I needed that I **could** recover, and it gave me the tools which were necessary to ensure that I **would** recover. There are so many people who **do** recover from M.E. (my favourite book which I recommend everyone with this illness should get is 'Recovery from M.E. 50 success stories' compiled by Alexandra Barton) and doing the course helped me realise this. I think that we can be more focused when we first start discovering about M.E. on the people who **don't** recover, and I think this can have a very detrimental effect on us. I think that for a lot of people who do recover from M.E. it can be quite scary to talk about it and share your story publicly, for fear of bringing it back. I know I have found this book difficult to write at times, because it has been so thorough, and I have felt so many emotions show up in my body. I genuinely believe and hope though, that by sharing my story, I can help provide hope to others. I feel it is so important that people are aware that you **can** recover.

I am so grateful for the people who do run these courses because they offer so much support to people who are struggling. Of course, the unfortunate thing here is that these courses aren't usually free. While you can get support through your GP and go to CFS specialists, appointments tend to be few and far between. I really hope that in the future, there is much more support available for people with this illness. I do think that with the arrival of Long-Covid, this may be more of a possibility, and I truly hope so. It is heart-breaking how many people go through this feeling alone and unable to get the support they need.

While I appreciate that not everyone may be able to afford one of the courses available, I would certainly encourage you to investigate them and consider one. My advice would be that if you do go for a course, please be prepared to **do** what they suggest. Give it your all (and I know of course, that your 'all' is limited when you are so ill) and commit to yourself. I did find that because I had paid out for the course, it made me that little bit more determined to stick with it. I am so glad that I did, as I think that without doing this, I would have been unwell for a lot longer, maybe even always been ill. The course encouraged me to take **control** back of my life, and that is what helped me to change my life for the better.

COUNSELLING

Counselling really helped me through this illness. I think it is such a shame that people are frightened of admitting they see a counsellor or feel any kind of shame about doing so. It is completely expected that when you are unwell or have an accident, you visit a doctor and ask for treatment of some sort. It would be great if it was just as acceptable that sometimes you may need that additional support from speaking to a counsellor/therapist.

I realised that I wasn't dealing with things as well as I could, which is completely understandable. I had been given a diagnosis of a life changing illness and advised that there was no cure, no official treatment and that I should actually expect to never fully recover from it. I was told that the best I could hope for was to learn to manage it, and that it was expected that I would get worse. When the enormity of all that sinks in, it can be so devastating. Of course, you can reach out for support from loved ones, but even that can cause issues. Even though I know I shouldn't have felt like I was a burden to my loved ones, I *did* feel that way. I had gone from being a 100 miles an hour mum/wife/friend/ employee/ volunteer... to being someone who sometimes couldn't walk, talk, or get out of bed. It was horrific. My immediate family had to live with it at home, and there were a few family members and close friends who supported me at certain times with physical things. I found that I didn't always want to talk about how I was feeling. I didn't want to add worries onto what everyone else was already having to deal with. So, I ended up keeping a lot of it in... which didn't do me any good. I truly believe it made me more ill, as all of those trapped emotions add toxicity to an already overworked, exhausted body and mind.

I ended up seeing three different therapists during my illness. I initially had sessions with Malcolm who ran the M.E. course at The Sanctuary of Healing, as he was a trained psychotherapist. This helped me see that I really did need to deal with things which I had been bottling up for years and telling myself I had dealt with. One amazing lady Stina, who I was able to have online calls with due to the Covid pandemic when we weren't allowed out of the house, and then later a wonderful man David who was able to come to our house. I will also add here that it is worth considering that counselling may be worth thinking about for people who are supporting you. We had David speak to all of us as a family, and then individually too. We had a time where Jack broke down and admitted that he was panicking all the time that we were keeping a secret from him. He thought I was dying as he said there was no way I could be so ill, with the doctors unable to help me, and clearly getting worse. It was absolutely heart breaking and made me realise that, as a parent, I had a duty to do whatever I could to try and help take that fear away. Obviously, I couldn't just 'magic' myself better, so James and I realised that it was worthwhile having somebody independent come in to speak to all of us. We wanted the children to be able to talk to someone about any of their worries and receive professional advice, without worrying about worrying us! This is one of the problems we humans have... we worry about worrying our loved ones, so we keep things in. Of course, that is only ever going to be detrimental to our own health, so it is always worth looking into the option of accessing some sort of counselling service.

Having a safe space to talk to someone meant so much to me. Although it took some getting used to, once I knew that I was ok to talk about absolutely anything, it helped me feel so much better. I could share fears and worries that I didn't always want to talk about with a loved one. I could voice concerns without being upset thinking that I was adding to someone else's worries. I could work out things myself with assistance, because it was better to say things out loud which I had been trying to keep inside. Sometimes just hearing myself say things aloud meant that I could rationalise them in a completely different way to when I was simply sat thinking and dwelling about them.

I realised during these sessions that I was still struggling to 'accept' the illness. Although I knew I was ill, I was still trying to **fight** it. Everyone says that you are a 'fighter' or a 'warrior' and that you are 'battling' the illness... and in some cases this may be right. I certainly felt like I was battling. However, I realised that I was trying to fight my own body, and that wasn't what my body needed. It needed me to be kind to it, rather than be in a huge, horrible fight with it all the time. While every day seemed like a battle, just to get through it the best I could, that didn't mean I should be battling my body. It clicked that I needed to treat myself very differently to how I was doing. I don't think I would have come up with that realisation without the help of an outside party who allowed me to talk through everything. Speaking to a counsellor isn't about getting someone else to fix your problems... nobody else can *fix* your problems! You must learn how to be strong enough to fix your own! But that doesn't mean you have to go through it alone! If you're struggling to get everything out of your system that you need to emotionally, then it is always worth considering speaking to a professional.

I think that people assume that in order to speak to a counsellor you need to be either struggling with mental health issues, or have experienced some sort of exceptional trauma. Firstly, let me tell you, being diagnosed with a life changing illness such as M.E. **is** a trauma. It can be extra hard in some ways because not everyone will take you seriously. People may unfortunately think that it's 'just tiredness' or assume that it isn't 'that bad'. They may see you out and about, if you are able to do that, and assume that you must be better. God forbid you go out and enjoy yourself because then of **course** you must have recovered and shouldn't have anything to complain about (they don't see the pain behind the smile, the rest you had to have before you went out and the repercussions of having done something, which could mean days, or weeks in bed recovering). It can feel so refreshing to talk to someone who you know won't be judging you, isn't personally involved with you and so will help to support you in a truly logical way.

I am open about seeing a counsellor because I found it so helpful, and I don't think there should be any stigma on doing it. If you needed surgery, you would see a surgeon. If you need counselling about an issue you are having trouble with, then it figures that you should consider seeing a counsellor! It really is that simple. The more people are ok to talk about it, the faster the stigma will go. I didn't have any specific mental health issues as such when I had my sessions, but it really, really doesn't matter whether you do or you don't. If truth be told, I think the act of seeing a counsellor may have helped to *stop* me having future mental health issues because I was able to process my emotions in a healthy way. I would certainly recommend it to anyone and everyone. Whether you are ill or not, most people will benefit from speaking to someone who is there solely to help support them in a non-judgemental and non-emotional way. It is also good if you are helping to support someone yourself, as I know from our experience as a family, that we were **all** having to deal with this horrible, traumatic illness, and all worrying about our own worries affecting each other! What a vicious cycle when you think about it!

A word of warning if you do decide to consider doing this (and I do hope that you do) ... it can be exhausting! I know it may not feel like the best thing to do to promote something which will exhaust you more than you already are, but I really feel it is worth it. It is also worth noting that while you may go in with the issue of being ill, you may end up unearthing different things from the past or even from now, which may cause more upheaval. It is important that you have extra support around you if possible after your sessions and that you are very, very kind to yourself. There were times I couldn't manage a full session because I was just too tired to talk. Zoom calls were great for me in a lot of ways because although I always tried to be dressed and sat up for them, this wasn't a pre-requisite. I guess one thing about the Covid pandemic is that so many more people are working from home now, including counsellors, so access is much more readily available for people who can't leave the house, or even leave their bed!

It is certainly worth speaking to your GP about it too, as they may be able to help support you with this. They may be able to refer you to an appropriate person.

One of the best things I have done for myself during this illness and my subsequent recovery, is to learn more about myself as a person and be able to deal with things differently. I no longer want to hold on to the past, or to be concerned about my future – I want to live in the present and enjoy my life for what it is. Having therapy has really helped me to do this – and even now I still have sessions which help me. I know that looking after my mental health is of the utmost importance in keeping my whole self well.

Part of my recovery has been me dealing with buried traumas from my past. I truly believe that if I had not done this, I would not have got better. Healing is not a straight line. It is messy, uncomfortable, and even painful at times. We often don't want to deal with traumatic incidents and so we do our best to try and bury them.

The thing is though, once we have experienced something, the emotions are there – and will stay trapped in your body, unless you actively choose to work on releasing them so you can truly move on.

While you may not want to re-visit old hurts (for obvious reasons), I really believe that it is of vital importance to assist you in moving past this illness. I have had several traumatic things happen in my life and I tried to tell myself that I was ok with them. I clearly wasn't – and I'm pretty sure that they all contributed towards me having M.E. Dealing with them has certainly had a huge impact on my recovery.

MEDITATION

Meditation has been a huge part of my journey to recovery, and I am so glad that I decided to commit to myself and make it a part of my every day life. Meditation is so very simple in some ways, and yet can be so difficult in others. Meditation and mindfulness are talked about much more recently, even though they have been around forever in one way or another. Anyone and everyone is capable of doing it, and there are so many people who recommend it; from everyday people like me, to celebrities, and even CEOs of multi-million-pound companies.

It's funny whenever I bring up meditation to people, the different reactions I can get. There can sadly be a lot of negativity around it, with people telling themselves that they simply can't do it, for one reason or another. Excuses I have heard have ranged from "I don't have the time", " I've tried it a couple of times and it's just not for me", "I can't clear my mind", "It makes my overthinking worse", " I can't stay still for that long", "I don't actually know what I'm doing", "I can't sit cross-legged", and even "I don't like the music you get with it."

Before you think I'm going all Judgy McJudge (which is my nickname for myself when I feel that I'm slipping into judgement zone (and let's be honest, we *all* judge at times)), then let me assure you that I have said or thought almost all of these excuses too! The great thing is, when you recognise that all these truly are just excuses, you can move forward and consider giving mediation a go.

You have probably heard about why meditation is good for you because it has been much more regularly publicised recently. It can be hard to accept that something so simple can have so many great effects, but it really can! Benefits such as reducing stress, anxiety and even depression. It can help to reduce pain, can lower the risk of illness, improve your emotional well-being, and even affect your memory in a positive way. It will encourage kindness and compassion, for yourself and for others. It is an amazing act of self-love, as you are giving yourself dedicated time out for yourself which will be helping you in numerous ways. It can help you sleep better; can help you feel better during the day and even help in the fight against addictions! The effects on the body can be quite incredible and it has even been shown to help reduce blood pressure! All of these amazing things... for something which is free, can be done literally anywhere and doesn't even need any type of specialist equipment! It really is incredible that not everybody is choosing to do it!

So, I guess the question is **why** is everyone not choosing to do it? Personally, I think that in the past people have related meditation to being a bit 'out there'. People haven't always understood what it is about and have maybe thought it is more complicated than it really is. They have assumed that you must sit cross-legged with a ramrod straight back, chanting unintelligible words and reaching a zen like state that they don't think would be possible for themselves. People often think that you must spend hours and hours doing it, dedicating time which you don't have to a practice you aren't even sure will do anything. They may think that you must be some sort of 'guru' or be a totally different type of person to who they are. And the big one (the one I found myself most inclined to think) was thinking that you had to know how to fully clear your mind.

My mind has always gone ten to the dozen. I was a huge overthinker, and worrier, with a mind that never switched off. I struggled to get to sleep, partly because my brain was so active at night. I would be in conversation with someone, but not fully present, as I would be dwelling about what they may be thinking of me. Even when I had any quiet time, my mind wouldn't switch off. If I was lucky enough to have, for example, a massage, I would be lay there worrying about something (including what the therapist was thinking about the sight of my semi naked body) rather than fully relaxing. So when I used to hear people talking about how much mediation was working wonders for them, I told myself the biggest lie (and one which I think lots of us are guilty of telling ourselves) "I just can't do that."

I had written something off without even giving it a proper try! Of course, I had tried it a couple of times, half-heartedly, and with the expectation that I wouldn't be able to do it (which of course is never the right attitude to go into with anything you want to do). Unsurprisingly, I hadn't been successful and had given up pretty much straightaway. It makes me sad now that I wasn't willing to give something which has so many proven benefits a try, just because I was too busy telling myself that it wasn't for me.

When you decide that you want to change your life in any way, you must be prepared to make the necessary changes, and you have to commit to yourself. It can never be enough to just try something once or twice, not get the hang of it straightaway and simply give it up as a bad job. You must give it a proper chance, otherwise you are doing yourself a real disservice. If you want to control your diet for whatever reason but then give up after two days, you will never see the results you wanted. If you decide to get fit and join a gym, but only go for a few sessions, then don't go back, you won't achieve the healthy body you yearn for. It is the same with your mind. If you wish to have a clearer mind, one which makes you feel better all-over, then you have to commit to yourself to do what it takes to get that result. Meditation truly is one of the things that you can do for your own mind. When your mind feels better, the rest of your life will feel so much better as a result!

All the research I had done into my illness, as well as all of the self-development I was doing, pointed me towards meditation. So many people were saying how helpful it was for so many reasons. It made complete sense for me to try it. Not just to try it though, but to **commit** to it. As I will always say, whenever you decide to commit to doing something helpful, you are making a commitment to yourself. I don't think you can do any better than that.

As with everything else I committed to when I made my decision to change my life, I decided to do a daily practice of meditation for a minimum of six months. I knew that if I wanted the best results, I couldn't just play around and try to fit it in here and there. It needed to be a daily commitment. I am so glad I did.

I won't lie; I found it difficult to start with. I wanted my mind to be clear straightaway. I wanted that 'quick fix'. I wanted a fairy wand to suddenly make it so that my mind would be magically clear of all thoughts so that I would somehow get what all the fuss was about in an instant. I wanted to be able to be grounded and clear headed with the minimum effort! I'll tell you now... that didn't happen for me (I would love it to happen for you... but I think that would probably be quite rare and I think we should be realistic here).

My mind didn't go quiet like I had wanted to. If you try meditation or have tried it in the past and experience the same, then I want to tell you something important. One thing I was taught (by a monk at a meditation day retreat no less, six whole months into my own meditation journey) was this...

YOUR MIND DOES NOT NEED TO BE SILENT TO MEDITATE.

What?

But surely that was what I was aiming for? Complete and utter stillness and silence?? So, here was this Buddhist monk telling me otherwise. Suddenly, everything clicked into place, and I felt my whole body heave a huge sigh of relief and then relax. I wish that I had heard someone say that before. I hope that when you read this, that you will firstly trust me when I say I have found it to be true through experience, and secondly that it will make you reconsider giving meditation a go (I promise you that it **is** worth it).

If you are getting started with meditation, I would highly recommend that you give guided meditation a go. I found that if I tried simply sitting in silence, I was trying to force it and it just didn't work for me. I would often end up more stressed than before I started, as I couldn't silence my mind. I would end up thinking negative and unhelpful thoughts, as I would tell myself that I was a failure at it. With guided meditations, you are guided through stages. Things like taking deep breaths, focusing on your breathing, and noticing certain things are all encouraged. When you listen, they are all obvious things to do... but when you don't practice these activities regularly, they are not always as natural as they could be.

There are guided meditations free on the internet, so you don't even have to pay a thing (unless you choose to). There are groups both online and in person which do them and there are even courses which help guide you through. I personally use an app on my phone. I am currently using the free Insight Timer app and love it as you can start from as little as a five-minute meditation There are so many guided meditations on there, as well as unguided ones where you can simply set a timer. There are meditations for a whole variety of different issues... from pain, grief, anger, eating, anxiety... the list is endless! They also have children's meditations which I love as I do them some evenings now at bedtime with the kids, which can be helpful for them.

I love that you can mediate wherever and whenever you want to. Learning to just be able to breathe deeply and go inwards, even for a minute, has proved invaluable to me whenever I am in a stressful situation. Let's face it, none of us can avoid stressful situations; we can just choose to handle them differently! Meditation means that I can now deal with things far better than I used to... and the impact can be seen not just on me, but also on my family, which is brilliant. I meditate and practice mindfulness every single day. Most days I do at least 20 minutes, sometimes more, but sometimes less. I tend to do at least one guided mediation a day as I really love them, but also try to slot in other times to do it where I can, as it really does have such a positive impact on me. I can meditate in bed, in the shower/bath, in the car (**not** when driving though of course), sitting down in the house...and I certainly practice mindfulness more whenever I am doing activities in the house or just out for a walk with my dog, Chewy. It's amazing to be able to have so much more control over my mind and I feel so much better for it.

Some days, like with most things, are better than others. Some days I feel so connected with what I am doing that I could spend hours on it, some days I don't feel that connected and my mind may stay busy. Some days life gets in the way, and I will go a full day and realise that I haven't given myself the time I need (and deserve, as we *all* do) to sit/lie down and meditate. I will always ensure then that I do a meditation in bed. To be honest, I go to sleep nearly every night now to a sleep meditation. I also listen to Yoga Nidra meditations which are fantastic for helping me get to sleep – or even helping to reset my energy or to heal during the day.

I really feel that when you learn to meditate, you should commit to giving it a good chance. I set myself six months as it was obviously part of what I was doing in my recovery. As I've said (a few times now), those six months would be happening anyway, so what's the harm in committing to something which is proven to help you?! For me, it's a no brainer! Especially when it is something which is free, doesn't need to take up hours of your time, can be done anywhere (and everywhere!) and is so highly recommended by professionals everywhere! You can do it on your own, or even take part in group meditations. For me, it is far better to work on your mind each day, rather than spend time filling your mind with junk! With it being so popular and publicised now, there has never been an easier time to get started with it.

AFFIRMATIONS

Whether you have never heard of affirmations, have a bit of an idea about them, or are an expert, I can guarantee that you will all be **doing** affirmations every single day. Yes...even if you haven't even a clue what the word means!

In simple terms, an affirmation is something you tell yourself, whether in thought or aloud. You can have positive/helpful affirmations, or negative/harmful affirmations. They are things you can tell yourself every day which can have a huge impact on you.

Have a look through the lists below and see whether you tell yourself any of these affirmations...

I am amazing.

I am a wonderful parent/spouse/friend.

I am great at my job.

I am happy and healthy.

I am strong and capable.

I am intelligent.

I can stick up for myself.

I am proud of myself for all that I have achieved.

I deserve only the best things in life.

Good things always happen to me, and I expect them to keep happening.

My body is in great shape.

I am physically attractive and always feel good about myself.

I am brave.

I can deal with anything life throws at me.

I am enough, exactly as I am.

People love me.

I love me.

Or how about these ones?...

I am rubbish.

I always mess up.

I am ugly/fat/unattractive.

I'm not as good as someone else.

I'm such a bad parent/spouse/friend.

I'm so thick.

I feel like a failure.

I'm pathetic.

I'm worried about what other people think of me.

I look such a mess.

I will never be good at this.

I don't know what I'm doing.

I can't do this.

I hate myself/my life/my body.

I wonder which list you could relate to the most? I'm praying that it's the first one, but, if you are anything like I used to be, then the second list may hit home a little. And while you think you may not be 'doing' affirmations, my guess is that you have told yourself some of these from the lists above at some point. Actually, you are likely to be doing them every day.

When I committed to my recovery, I committed to doing daily affirmations. I had heard of them before my recovery attempt and had even given them a little bit of a try but told myself (actually I affirmed!) that 'this isn't really for me'. I didn't commit to a daily practice as I didn't really see how they could really work, so I gave up.

I then discovered Louise Hay. If you have never heard of her or read/listened to any of her books/work, then can I highly recommend that you do. She was very ill herself (with cancer) and managed to heal herself. She put a huge onus on positive affirmations helping her to do that. I listened to her book, then bought myself a hard copy as I loved it so much. I then decided to commit to the practice of repeating positive affirmations every day for... you've guessed it, six months!

Our minds and bodies are so linked, much more than a lot of people will realise. It is no coincidence that if we are feeling uneasy in our minds, our bodies will struggle too. If you are anxious about something, you may feel it in the 'pit of your stomach'. When you feel mentally in a good place, it's highly likely that your body will feel good. If you aren't feeling mentally great, then your body may feel pretty rubbish. It makes complete sense then that you should try your best to put as much goodness into your mind as possible. Doing this means that your mind **and** your body will feel good! This is where affirmations can play an important part.

If you are always being unkind to yourself and telling yourself negative things, then you are not very likely to feel good about yourself. Nobody likes to be berated... and yet so often we do it to ourselves. Imagine how bad you would feel if someone you know was being horrible to you. Imagine if your boss calls you out for doing a bad job; or your spouse tells you that you aren't looking your best; or your kids tell you that you are a rubbish parent; or a friend tells you that you aren't good enough for them; or a stranger says that you must be completely stupid! In some cases, you wouldn't stand for it! How often do we do this to ourselves though? It's so sad! We should be nourishing our minds with kind words, rather than punishing them with unkind ones. You are with yourself 24 hours a day, every single day of your life! You may be able to escape from someone else who puts you down...but you can't escape from yourself! Therefore, it's vitally important that you learn to speak kindly to yourself.

While it may take some time to get used to telling yourself nice things, it will certainly have a positive effect on you. It may seem strange telling yourself that you love yourself... but it is better than telling yourself that you hate yourself. If you wouldn't say it to someone else, you really shouldn't be saying it to yourself!

When I got started with affirmations, I felt like some of them were lies. I genuinely felt like I would be lying to myself if I was saying some of the things I saw recommended in books. I was so ill, and I had got caught in the trap of reiterating to myself every day that I was ill. It felt completely alien to suddenly try to change my thinking and tell myself that I wasn't ill but was actually strong and healthy. I figured that I wanted to **be** strong and healthy though, and so it made sense to tell my mind those things, rather than keep on focusing on being ill. I figured that if I kept telling myself the positive affirmations, kept putting the work in to try and make it happen, and believed that it would come true... then there was a bigger chance of it coming true than if I was sitting in bed telling myself every day that I was still unwell.

I found loads of affirmations and initially went a bit gung-ho with them, repeating lots of different ones. However, something didn't feel quite right, and I had to sit down and work out what wasn't working for me. I realised that I wasn't being specific with what I wanted. I needed to be clear about what I wanted the most. There are affirmations for literally everything and so it's very easy to simply repeat a load, but it's far better (in my opinion) to find ones which resonate personally with you. I really focused on what I wanted in my life and came up with my own personal affirmations which felt right for *me*. I decided it would be far better to repeat these as many times as I could. I opted to focus on saying "I am happy. I am healthy. All is well." In fact, I went a bit further with this and ended up making a song! Yes, I'm very random, but trust me, it helped as it got stuck in my head! It made me laugh and so even when I was feeling down, I would sing my little affirmation song, and it truly did help me feel that little bit brighter. And even 1% brighter every day is better, right?!

In case you are wondering how my song goes, I will of course let you know! I sing it to the tune of "She'll be coming round the mountain when she comes." It goes like this...

"I am happy, I am healthy, all is well. I am happy, I am healthy, all is well. I am happy, happy, happy. I am healthy, healthy, healthy. I am happy, I am healthy, all is well."

I have taught my kids about affirmations (along with lots of the other things that I have done/am doing on my journey) and they absolutely love this song! We all sing it together and it really makes me so happy! In fact, I have three plaques up around the house now with these words engraved on them, and even a set of coasters my husband had made up which state 'Pods are happy, Pods are healthy, Pods are well.'

I repeat this to myself, in my head and out loud, every single day, many times a day! In fact, whenever I can feel any negativity creep in, or any symptoms flare up, or even when my mind is feeling overwhelmed with things, I stop and sing this. Does it magic things better? Yes and no. Of course, I still have whatever I am dealing with to deal with, but I just feel that little bit brighter and stronger in myself. That makes things a little bit easier to deal with. And if that's not some sort of magic, then I don't know what is.

I genuinely feel that doing this work has helped me in so many ways. I use affirmations every day. I have a favourite Louise Hay 30 minutes of affirmations audiobook I listen to called 'Love Your Body'. When I was initially in recovery, I listened to this every single day. I love listening to books/podcasts etc, as you can literally listen to them anywhere. I still listen to this particular one regularly because it truly is so good and I believe it's far better to fill your mind with helpful things, rather than allowing it to be filled with harmful things each day. I listen to it when I'm walking the dog, driving on my own (and sometimes even with the kids... they do laugh at a couple of words she says, as did I when I first listened... I won't spoil it for you), doing housework, lying in bed, having a bath, cooking tea... it really is something you can do at a huge variety of times and places.

Whether you tell yourself 'good' things or 'bad' things, you are flooding your body with chemicals. They can either be feel-good chemicals or feel-bad chemicals. When you think about it this way, it surely makes sense to *choose* to have the feel-good chemicals floating around. You may think that you don't have that much control over how you feel, but you **do!** Of course, you aren't going to feel amazing by saying a couple of affirmations every now and then! If only it were that simple! This needs to be something that you commit to. Like anything, the more you practice it, the more you will get used to it and the better you will become at it! Like someone taking up exercise, the stronger their body will become the more they do... the stronger your mind can become through doing these affirmations! It's something which **everyone** can do! It's free, it can literally take a few seconds, you don't need any specific training, and nobody need even know that you're doing it! This is why I truly believe everyone would benefit from giving them a go and try to get into the habit of doing them! While I appreciate that they may feel alien to you at first, they soon get easier to do. You are with yourself 24/7 and your mind rarely switches off! So why not choose to be kinder to your mind than you may be being right now? There is literally nothing stopping you being able to do this - other than you telling yourself that you can't for whatever reason!

I would suggest that you start off simply. Don't overwhelm yourself with lots of different affirmations. Find something which is personal to you. I know it can be hard getting started as you may not be sure what you should be saying. There really is no 'should' here though. You do what works for *you*. If you research affirmations, lots of examples will come up so that you can choose which ever ones resonate with you. Alternatively, you can even come up with some of your own. I have gone on to create a list of my own personal affirmations and I try to make sure that once a day I go through this list as they are perfect for **me**. They include things which would be suitable for most people, such as 'I am healthy' and then ones which wouldn't work for everyone, like 'I am a writer'.

It's worth finding which ones you really love and feel especially pertinent to you and then repeating those ones as many times as you can. Please feel free to try out my cheesy little "I am happy, I am healthy, all is well" song! I can guarantee that pretty much everyone wants these things in life (health and happiness) ... and when you have a little song like that, it can help you remember it that little bit more!

I say affirmations every morning and every night without fail as it is now such a strong habit for me. I have the plaques around the house, and I have my own personal list written out and kept in my bathroom so that I don't forget to do them (I choose to do them when I'm brushing my teeth). I also have an app on my phone called 'I Am' which sends me affirmations during the day. I love this as they are a constant reminder of how wonderful life is and they often come just as I need that little mental pick me up. I even post an affirmation every evening in my 'Positive Mind, Positive Life' group.

Sometimes, my mind still wants to argue about one of the affirmations if I've had a tough day, as it may feel like a lie to say out loud 'I am strong'. I may want to mentally argue back that "Well, I'm **not** really strong today though, am I?" but I make sure I catch myself. I remind myself that I can focus on the fact that I don't feel great, which will end up making me feel worse, or I can tell myself that I feel strong, and make my body that little bit happier.

When you realise how much power your own thoughts have, you certainly choose to think a different way! Thoughts lead to emotions and so can have a massive impact on our bodies. So, if you are actively choosing to think helpful thoughts, you are actively choosing to help your own mind and body. I'm aware it sounds too simple and good to be true... and yet this is how it is. I'm not saying you can think yourself well, because not everyone can do that (please note that I'm also not saying that you **can't** think yourself well, as I believe that with the right mindset, you may be able to do just that in certain cases), but I believe that's because people tell themselves they can't! As soon as that doubt has crept in about anything, you are telling yourself you can't.

Affirmations won't cure you. They won't make you all better overnight. They **will** however make your mind and body stronger if you commit to doing them! They are a great way to show yourself some self-love, which is something everyone can benefit from. It is something I want my children to do, so it makes sense that they follow my lead! You truly do have nothing to lose by giving them a go!

SELF-CARE

Self-care is talked and written about all the time now. It seems like everyone is talking about how important it is to participate in self-care, to 'look after yourself', to 'put yourself first', to 'make yourself a priority' and telling you that 'self-care isn't selfish'. I absolutely agree with all these statements of course... however I have noticed that quite often the people who talk about this the most, may be the ones who need to practice self-care the most. I certainly used to be one of those people. I thought that self-care was selfish. I thought it was all about taking long bubble baths, and even worse, about eating foods and drinking drinks which were damaging to my body.

We see images of 'self-care' being things which we may not have the time, money, or energy for. Long walks, weekends away, massages, spa days, meals out... they can certainly be out of reach for many of us. Even if you try to re-create a 'spa at home' in your own bathroom, you can guarantee that there will be someone knocking on the door as soon as you get in the bath!

The truth is though, that self-care is far simpler than that. It truly is about caring for yourself. That doesn't mean all the extravagant things you may initially think of... it can mean easy things. It means listening to your body and resting when you are tired. It means eating nourishing foods which make your body feel good from the inside. It means learning to quiet your mind so that you aren't always so overwhelmed with life. It means taking some time out for yourself so that you can do something which you enjoy. It means getting outside to walk, or maybe sit, in nature, even if it's only for a short time. It means plugging into something which makes you feel brighter. It means switching off from the negativity in the world. It can be a chat with a friend. It can be standing in front of a mirror and telling yourself nice things. It can be spending time with your favourite people. It can be listening to music which makes you feel good, and even dancing to it if you get the chance. It may even mean things like getting organised so that the week flows better. Or de-cluttering a room, or a drawer, so that you feel calmer when you see it. It is basically anything which makes you feel better about yourself and your life. That will look different to everyone. One person may love a bubble bath... but it could be someone else's idea of hell!

What is important for everyone, whether you are ill or not, is to practice self-care as much as possible. Quite often people will tell themselves that they haven't got the time for self-care, but even five minutes here or there during the day can make a big difference. Just taking five minutes to do some deep breathing exercises or taking yourself to a different place when you are feeling stressed can help you feel calmer. It is all about making your mind and body feel better. Of course, it is wonderful if you can manage an hour, or even longer each day to yourself, but I appreciate that not everyone will always have that opportunity. What I realised is that, in the past, even if I **did** have the opportunity, I would feel bad for doing something for myself. I wouldn't make the most of time to myself, but instead would do something which I thought I 'should' be doing, rather than what I would like to be doing! Once I realised that this wasn't truly benefitting others though, I made a conscious decision to incorporate self-care into my daily routine. It's all well and good helping everyone else, but if you aren't caring for yourself properly, you may end up burning out. This then leaves you unable to help other people. I hated being so ill that I couldn't help others, but I had to accept that I had to say no more often. Even now, I make sure that I still do that when necessary for my own health and well-being. It's lovely being able to do more for others now and I'm delighted to even be in a position to volunteer again. I know my limits though, and if I have to say no, I do. Even if it means letting other people down. I'm aware that may sound harsh and obviously I would never want to leave anyone in the lurch, but if I know that I'm struggling myself, it's not great to do something for someone else which could ultimately result in me becoming unwell.

I am now strong enough in myself to let people know that my self-care is a priority. My family know that if I'm saying no to something, it's because I am protecting myself and putting my health and wellness first. I will let my kids know that I am taking time out for myself, and they know that it is important that they allow me to do that, without them bothering me. (I love my kids... but any parent knows that feeling of getting into a bath to hear 'mummmmmeeeeeeee/dadddddeeeeeee', accompanied by that sinking feeling and wishing that you could just be left alone for a while.) I'm glad that my children see first-hand how important self-care is, because one of my worst fears is that they don't look after themselves properly when they are older and end up burning out or becoming ill. I want them to grow up knowing that it's more than ok to put yourself first, to say no and to take time out to do things that you enjoy. Of course, they also know about compromise and that sometimes we must sacrifice things for others... but ultimately, I do not want either of them overdoing things. They would have learned from me that you put everyone else first, even if that is to the detriment of your own health, if I had carried on the way I was before getting M.E. I sometimes wonder (hope) if me getting ill may help to prevent them from doing the same in the future.

Practicing self-care means that I have stopped putting myself under unnecessary pressure. My expectations of myself have always been pretty high (which I think is a common theme for people who end up with M.E.) I always felt like I could, and **should**, be doing more. I now know that it is far better to keep a steadier pace and enjoy myself more by being present in the moment, rather than always worrying about what I was doing next as I had so much on.

It is also important to learn how to deal with your emotions. I felt so many different emotions when I was so unwell... and I'm aware that everyone deals with so many emotions whether you are ill or not. When we are children, we don't focus about suppressing these feelings, we simply say what we feel and react accordingly.

But we are then taught that we need to keep quiet; don't cry; don't show yourself up in public; put a brave face on. We may feel that it's weak to be emotional and so we learn to keep our feelings hidden. This can mean though that sometimes we don't even allow ourselves to deal with things properly and this can be so detrimental to our health. Society seems to have a certain acceptance level of different things. Even when someone dies, people may think that a person grieving should be able to move on after a certain amount of time and so we can feel pressure to not talk about how we are really feeling, for fear of judgement.

Part of caring for yourself is giving yourself chance to properly deal with your emotions so that they don't stay bottled up and end up manifesting themselves as physical symptoms in your body later. Taking time out for yourself and working out how you are feeling about certain situations will always be beneficial. Going on to take appropriate action will help too.

I also fully recommend looking at the things you watch, read and listen to each day. I choose to fill my mind with as much positivity as I can. It's ironic that something as positive as 'being positive' has now ended up being criticised by some people. I fully agree that we shouldn't be plastering fake smiles on our faces no matter how we feel, or telling the world we feel wonderful, or even just ok, when we are struggling just to get through each day. That's doesn't do anyone any good. But I truly believe that if you can find good things to focus on, it will always far outweigh only focusing on the bad things!

I choose to regularly be listening to an audio book which is helping me work on my mindset. Likewise, I read books which help me do the same. I have got a book and/or an audiobook on the go every single day. I love that my mind is always being filled with things which not only make me feel good, but also make me **want** to make the most of myself. My views on a few things have certainly changed since being ill and I am a much more open person than I used to be. I have done several courses which have helped me and will continue to do more. I really believe that M.E. has made me become a different person in several ways, and I don't see that as a bad thing anymore. I never would have practised self-care the way I do now if I hadn't got so ill. I would have continued to take on too much and would have carried on being run down a lot of the time. I would have kept things bottled up and been too worried about what other people thought of me to say no to things which I didn't want to do. Keeping my mindset strong is one of the best things I will ever do for myself, and I have made the commitment to ensure it is a daily practice.

Self-care isn't selfish. It truly is a selfless act which gives far more to you and your loved ones than pushing yourself to the point of exhaustion ever will!

CUTTING DOWN ON TV, THE NEWS & SOCIAL MEDIA

This may be something which causes a bit of an uncomfortable feeling when you think about doing it, because we have come to rely on social media and the television so much – especially if you are ill and cannot connect with other people and the outside world in the same way you used to. When I did the ANS Rewire Course, it recommended cutting down on, or even cutting out, certain things which may trigger your ANS... and when I really thought about it, it made so much sense.

I realised that I needed to rest **properly**. That didn't just mean resting my body... it meant resting my brain and my mind too. There was no good lying in bed or having a soak in the bath, while my mind was working overtime because I was scrolling through social media or watching something dramatic. So, I committed to massive cut downs on TV, internet use, being on my phone and social media usage. It all made a **big** difference.

I recently listened to a book by Alex Howard called Decode Your Fatigue. In it he describes a conversation he had with his uncle when he was suffering a lot with M.E. His uncle asked him to make a list of things which he knew made him worse (or were likely to make him feel worse), then to do a list of things which he knew would make him feel better (or were likely to make him feel better). He then asked him on a scale of 1-10 how much he **really** wanted to get better. Of course, Alex answered with a high number, as you would expect. However, when his uncle asked him what he was actually *doing* in order to aid his **own** recovery, he realised that he wasn't doing enough of the beneficial activities. He was also doing too many activities which would not aid his recovery, for example spending hours watching TV. That was a real eye opener for me again, as it made me think about how it was **me** who needed to take control of my own recovery and stop making excuses. I needed to be fully committed to doing *whatever* it took to try and get well again and be prepared to cut out doing anything which may end up making me feel worse. It sounds obvious, I know... and yet when you are in the depths of illness, it isn't always as simple as it sounds.

It's also quite difficult to be looking at having to, once again, give up things which you enjoy. I think that was one of the recurring things for me when I was coming to terms with the illness. I felt that I was having so much taken away from me and was having to give up so much. In all honesty, it didn't feel fair. Like a tantruming toddler, I wanted to stamp my foot and refuse to do certain things. It felt completely wrong that I had been forced to give up work, stop volunteering, lose my social life, stop being the mum/wife/friend I wanted to be, give up exercising... and now I was looking at having to give up the pleasures of TV, my phone, the internet, social media, and even reading and writing to some extent. I mean seriously... what on earth was I supposed to do?

The more I looked into it all though, the more it made complete sense to me. Again (I will always come back to this one common theme) mindset came into play with this. I realised that I had to do whatever I had to do. I had to be willing to do **whatever** it took to get better. It really was as simple as that. This was about **choice** now. A choice to try my best to recover, accepting that even if it didn't get the results I was hoping for, I knew that I would have given it my best shot and wouldn't be left wondering if there was anything else I could have tried. OR the choice was to not only accept the illness (which is a big part of dealing with the illness and must be done at some point in the journey) but to accept that I was helpless in my own recovery, and therefore helpless in my own life. Sometimes, the way you word or hear things can make all the difference. When I thought of it like that, then there really was no choice. I wanted my life back. I wanted to recover. I wanted to be pain and symptom free. I wanted to be well enough to not only survive, but to *thrive*. I was prepared to give it my all.

I knew that I needed to be doing everything within my power to help myself. That's an important thing with this illness (and with other things in life I know) ... feeling like you have actual power and control over what is going on in your own life. M.E. had made me feel powerless. I wanted to have some power in my life again. I knew that everything I was doing was also good for me. I wasn't doing anything which could make me feel worse, and my hope was that it would all start to work for me and make me feel better. I had nothing to lose.

One of the best things about giving up or reducing your daily intake of technological entertainment in the hopes that it will help you recover, is that it is free! Having M.E. can cost a small fortune when you are constantly trying new things and making so many changes, so it felt good that I had found something else which didn't cost me a lot of money. (I love to find positives in as many things as I can.)

I initially worried that if I didn't have my phone, social media, and TV, I may end up going stir crazy. How would I be able to keep myself occupied? Especially on days where I couldn't even get out of bed without needing help from James. I was concerned that I was taking myself away from one of the things I was able to do with my family, even on my worst days. (This is where I made my concession with watching TV as I would still choose to watch family films with my children at the weekend... but they would have to be very strictly family friendly, with nothing which was likely to trigger my ANS.)

However, doing this was certainly worthwhile and had amazing results for me. I was allowing my brain and my mind proper time to switch off. We are so overloaded with information now. For me (and I'm sure for many others) my phone was previously often in my hand from first thing in the morning, until last thing at night. It was relentless... and yet completely of my own choosing. I do believe now that I became obsessed with my phone, and I think that many of us may be able to relate to this. I did not even enjoy all the time I spent watching TV, or listening to/watching the news, or scrolling through social media - yet I would still choose to do it. Every day, and every night! It makes me wonder now when did this happen? When did it become the norm that we made such attachments to electronic devices?

I realised that doing all those things were actually making me fairly miserable. When I sat and thought about the types of TV programmes I was watching, I saw that I was affecting my own body in a negative way. When you are watching something which is full of violence, grief, and drama (and let's face it, most of the stuff out there at the minute is full of it), then it will of course affect our minds... and our bodies in turn. I realised that I was keeping my body in a high state of anxiety, just through my choices of what I was putting into my mind and watching.

There are still programmes which I watched in the past which make me feel emotional even now. I remember watching an awful programme about a father who had killed his family when he began an affair... and it really affected me. To the point that even a couple of years later it will occasionally pop into my head. And then, I feel it in my body. It isn't just that I feel sad, my whole body is affected, and it doesn't feel good at all. (I look back and sometimes wonder how on earth I manged to stay in the job I did for so long, when a TV programme can affect me so much.)

When you learn how to listen to your body properly, you can tell the effects your emotions have on it. You can literally put this to the test right now. Simply close your eyes and think about something which makes you feel a strong emotion... then see what happens inside (or even outside) your body. You may have a tight chest, your breathing may change, you may feel worse in yourself (or better if it's a good emotion), your hands may become sweaty, you may even feel pain in certain parts of your body.

Imagine, that you may be doing all this to yourself... just by watching TV! When I realised that, I knew that this (like pretty much everything else I was doing in these initial six months) needed to be a lifetime change. Genuinely, I'm 100% fine with this. I would now not choose to watch something which is going to make me feel rubbish. Don't get me wrong, I know that there will be times I'm tempted. If they do another series of Line of Duty, then I may debate with myself as to whether I should watch it. I may even discuss the pros and cons with James. But ultimately, I guess I already know what the answer will be. I know that if I watch it, I may end up making myself feel worse. Like it or not, one thing I have had to accept with this illness, is that my body knows how to **protect** itself and if I choose not to look after it to the best of my ability, I may end up suffering! I enjoy my pain and symptom free life *far* too much to want to risk losing it, for the sake of watching a show on TV.

Although I have never been a particular avid news watcher, I found that during my illness (partly of course because of the Covid pandemic when I think so many of us tuned in to see what was happening) I was following the news much more. I had a news app on my phone and would check it in the morning, then even found myself checking it regularly during the day. This did absolutely *nothing* for my wellbeing! In fact, I think everyone can see how being tuned into the news regularly can have a detrimental effect on your health, whether you are ill or not. The news is flooded with negativity. Positive news simply doesn't sell. Of course, you can choose to find good news stories... and most news companies will try and put at least one good story on, but you must wade through all the negative stuff to get to that one snippet of a happy story. Connecting with the news each day is not beneficial for your mindset, and certainly not good for your physical health either, as there is such a strong link between mind and body which we know to be true now. If you are watching the news, you are allowing yourself to become bogged down with the sadness, and even badness, of what is happening in the world, on a local and on a global scale.

Now, while I'm not suggesting that you remain completely ignorant of the world and never check in with what is going on in the news, it's really important to consider how much you are currently seeing on a daily basis. Cutting out the news had a big impact on me. Again, it was something which I had become a little obsessed with, and even now, when I pick up my phone, I can sometimes feel the urge to just check the headlines. I know that my life has been better from switching off from the news and I fully intend to keep it that way. I choose what goes into my mind now via the podcasts and audiobooks I listen to... rather than hearing about the atrocities in the world. I don't want to seem like I am completely naive as to what's going on, and I haven't been able to switch off 100% as I still have access to the news when I do go on social media via people's posts, or see headlines, or hear things on the radio; but I choose not to actively tune into it or dwell on it.

Prior to being ill, I had started with an online side business, and I did devote a lot of my 'spoons' to that, without realising that it was costing me far too much energy. As I was unable to physically work anymore, I really struggled emotionally as I felt like a failure. I just couldn't deal with the fact that I was no longer working. I felt worthless. It hurts my heart when I think about the pressure I put myself under, and I know that I am in no way alone in this. It is so hard when you have things taken from you due to ill health, and you do feel like part of your identity has gone. You feel judged by others when you can't work. Even worse, you may judge yourself. The mean girl inside me was very unkind about my inability to work.

I decided that at least I could still do my online business. I know now that it made me more unwell, even though at the time I thought that it was helping me. Don't get me wrong, I loved what I did, and I know that it works for a lot of people when they are ill. For a lot of people, it may even be a lifeline. In a way I guess it was for me for a while. I was on social media a lot and that stopped me feeling as lonely. Some of my friends had drifted off when I became unwell and I found new friends online who it didn't matter to if I wasn't well, as I didn't have to cancel plans with them.

I didn't realise how much harm I was doing myself by being on my phone so much though. I wasn't ever giving my brain a proper switch off. While I felt that I at least still had a purpose because I was still able to bring some money in, I failed to see that long term I was doing more damage to myself.

Social media has been a lifeline to me in so many ways, but it has also affected me mentally in so many ways too! This was one of the hardest things to deal with when I had to change my lifestyle. I was on it for a huge amount of time, partly of course because I was using it for work purposes… but also because I kept getting stuck in what is commonly known as the 'scroll hole'. You know, where you mean to nip on Facebook for five minutes before doing something else, only to find that you have somehow lost a full hour of your life scrolling through pictures of other people's lives? Now, while it can be nice to see what other people are getting up to, and connecting with people who you may not see physically very much (or even ever) anymore… there can also be a lot of drawbacks to being on social media. I truly can understand why so many people hate it, as it can cause so many problems. I have fallen privy to the pitfalls of Facebook myself so many times; seeing other people out and about when you are stuck in can be especially hard. Even though I was happy that other people were happy, I will never deny that I used to feel jealous. I used to be so envious of people with good health… especially when they seemed to take it for granted. I used to despair at people showing themselves pushing themselves to the limit but not being willing to accept help. I used to compare my life to everyone else's. There, in one sentence, is the major problem. We get caught up in the comparison game, and it can be so detrimental!

Now, I can accept that people use social media like a photo album. You would only ever pick the best pictures for a photo album, or to display on your wall; so why would social media be any different? Plus, unlike inviting people into your house where they can see the pictures, you are inviting the whole world (or even if not quite that, a lot more people than you may ever invite into your physical home) to have a look. Why wouldn't you want to tell the stories of you having a good time? Why wouldn't you choose the picture where you look the best (and discard the ones where you don't?) Long gone are the disposable cameras you had to wait two weeks to get your pictures back to find that you only had three decent photographs of yourself. While I'm not personally a fan of filters, I can totally understand why people choose to make themselves look that little bit brighter before sharing their pictures. The important thing to remember though, is that you only ever see a *snapshot* of anyone's life! You don't see the rest of the time, where they are doing the same as you and probably looking pretty ordinary too! You don't see the arguments, the anxiety, the break downs, or the day-to-day boring jobs; you simply see the glamorous bits that people want to share.

The content of social media can cause problems. There can be **so** much negativity on there. People complaining has always happened of course… and sometimes we need to be able to vent and talk about our issues! But the way social media is set up means that people can complain on and on and on. Then the debates start, and the nastiness, and the trolls. Insecure, unpleasant people who find enjoyment in making other people feel horrible with their awful comments. All of this means that going on social media can make for a miserable time if you aren't careful!

Initially, I found it hard to come off social media. It had become such a big part of my life. It was there for me 24/7. It didn't matter what I looked like, how I was feeling or whether I could do anything else. I found that I couldn't come off it fully at first. Gosh, it sounds crazy when I write that down and admit to how much of a hold it had on me... but I will only ever be honest about things. Also, as regretful as it may sound, I'm pretty sure that I won't actually be alone in it, as I'm well aware that things like Facebook are *designed* to be addictive.

Eventually, it got easier to be off social media. I would set myself limits so that I would only be on it for 5-10 minutes a couple of times a day. I stopped posting every day, I didn't spend hours commenting on other people's posts (this did mean that I lost a lot of interaction with people, but I knew that my health was much more important than that) and I stopped bothering about 'Facebook politics'.

I started to feel the difference quickly. I was focusing on **me** properly. For the first time in a very long time, if truth be told. I wasn't looking at what everyone else was doing, and so it couldn't affect or upset me. I realised that this was a far better way for me to be. My body certainly agreed. The more rest my body and mind got, the better I started to feel.

Even now when I'm so much better, I have to be very careful with social media. I can still feel the pull towards it if I'm honest and so am careful to try and set myself limits. Just the other day I wasn't really paying attention and suddenly found that an hour had gone by without me realising it. It hadn't been an hour of goodness either... it was literally just an hour of being stuck in the scroll hole and checking out comments on stupid adverts, and debates between people on different posts! Pretty pointless really!

I had to decide what I wanted from social media and stick to that. I didn't want to fully give it up, because I like the connections; I like to share my positivity; I like to chronicle some of my journey (I love seeing my memories pop up which remind of me of good times... as well as bad times, as they show me how far I have come through my illness). I also like to be part of certain groups which I find helpful for my recovery. When I first got diagnosed, I joined some M.E. groups (I will discuss this further on) and I have now focused on the ones which benefit me. I am in some positive post groups, which I love. I am also in some different nutritional and alternative healing groups, which currently serve a good purpose in helping me with knowledge and support. Of course, I am aware that as with anything, with people comes judgment. So even in these helpful groups, I make sure I don't spend too long in there and I avoid any topics which I know are likely to cause unhealthy debates. I still post on my feed regularly... but it feels like it's better content actually, as I'm no longer posting for the sake of posting. I also set up my own little group purely for positive posts (Positive Mind, Positive Life); I know I get a lot from similar groups, so I wanted my own group which helps me, and I hope also helps other people too. I share daily positive quotes and evening affirmations in there. The thing I love about this is being able to feel like I'm putting some goodness into the social media world, without it draining my own energy like it used to.

I am now so glad that I decided to commit to my recovery and remove all these things in my life which weren't serving a good purpose for me and were contributing to my ill health. Although the changes were difficult at first, the benefits have been amazing. So much so, that I will never go back to the way I was. I choose what I put into my mind now, as much as I can. Of course, it's not always possible to only have positive things going on, because the world will always have things going on which are likely to cause upset. There will always be things which are going to cause grief and pain.... death, relationship breakdowns, disease, failures, war, economic issues etc... but I know that I am in a much stronger place to be able to deal with any of these. By refusing to get caught up in all the little dramas which can end up taking over our lives at the time we are dealing with them, I'm saving myself, and my health, from being unnecessarily under any pressure or stress. To me, this is a far healthier way to live.

SUPPORT GROUPS

Having an illness like M.E. can certainly leave you feeling quite isolated, so I really think it is important to try and get as much support as you can. Unfortunately, and without meaning to sound pessimistic, you may find that you don't get as much support from some of the family members, friends, and colleagues that you would like or perhaps expect. M.E. is still not understood by a lot of people, and even worse, some people don't believe in it.

It can be tough when you feel that people don't support you. When you do find people who support you through it all, then those people are absolute legends. They deserve a lot of credit themselves, as I know it must be difficult supporting someone you know/love, without knowing whether they will ever get better.

It's hard when people don't understand how you are feeling. It's also hard when they say things which you know they mean well by which upset you. Please don't ever forget that sometimes people don't know what to say and may come out with ignorant things which may hurt you... even though that will never be their intention. I'm pretty sure we have all said things to people at some point (I know for a fact I have!) which end up being hurtful, even though we would never mean to hurt them. I do believe that most people don't choose to be ignorant of things, but unless you take the time to research something, or sit down and speak properly to someone about something they are experiencing, then you may not have the full picture. Personally, I know that I wasn't fully aware of what M.E. actually was before I got ill. I had a friend who had been diagnosed with it, but I still didn't understand it... because I didn't put the effort into finding out about it. Let's face it, there are so many illnesses out there, that none of us will ever be experts on all of them. I think unless you are personally affected by something, you are unlikely to take the time to sit and research the ins and outs of any particular illness. Obviously, when it does affect you individually in some way, it's important that you do take some time out to find out about it, even if only so that you can empathise with whoever has been affected a little bit more. You may never know what it feels like, but you will realise that saying things like "Oh I think I must have this M.E. thing you've got because I'm always pretty tired" may not be the best thing to say to someone who is so exhausted and in so much pain that even being awake can be painful beyond description.

If you find yourself ill and end up with less support than you may like, please don't feel that you **are** alone. What's important to remember, is that other people have things going on in their lives too. I know that may sound a bit harsh, but it is what I told myself when I was feeling left out, or sad that people had stopped contacting me. When I took it personally, it made me feel worse. The emotional flare up would set off my body pains and other symptoms. So genuinely, by allowing myself to focus on the fact that I was feeling unsupported by certain people, I was making myself feel more ill, and that truly wasn't worth it. Other people have so much going on in their own lives though, that it would actually be ignorant for you to think that you being unwell is going to take precedent in anyone's life but your own. Even now, if you sit and think for a minute of your own group of friends/family, most of those people will have issues of their own which you may be aware of. I can guarantee that there will be a lot more stuff going on that you **don't** necessarily know about. So please, please don't get caught up in the trap of feeling that you are unsupported by everyone.

Support groups can really help you. It can be beneficial to find people who can understand you, because they are unfortunately in a similar situation to you. With the rise of social media, this can be done within minutes! There are so many online groups now set up for people dealing with most illnesses. I know when I looked on Facebook alone, I found so many M.E. groups. I will give a word of warning here, as I fell afoul of this at the start. Beware of the groups where people sit around complaining. There is nothing worse than getting into threads where people are only focusing on the negatives. Or posts where people are comparing their symptoms in a way which make you feel bad about your own symptoms… either that you don't feel 'ill enough' to be in the group, so you start to feel self-doubt, or that you are clearly 'more ill' than most people in there and so you end up feeling extra sorry for yourself. While it really is important to know that you aren't alone, and it can be good to know that there are other people sharing similar experiences to you; it can be easy to slip into a negative mindset. This illness is horrible, there is no getting around that. But you need **support**… not a 'symptom off' (you know, a bit like a dance off, but where one person tries to out-do the other by showing how they are far more ill than everyone else! Before you mock that idea, trust me, it happens)!

My advice would be to find groups on social media which encourage people to support each other without you end up feeling worse than you did before you set (virtual) foot in the group. Look for groups which encourage talk of recovery and positivity. When you are so ill, it's important that you have faith that you **can** and **will** recover… so it's brilliant to find stories from people who are in the process of doing just that or have already done it.

How much you get involved in the groups is up to you of course. My advice would be to not spend too long on social media. It is vital that you are getting as much rest as you can, and even something which seems like it can be restful, is not always restful when you are ill. That took me a long time to work out of course, so know that I'm quite open about the fact that I did myself a disservice by being on social media so much for so long. I know it's hard to not get drawn into it. Maybe find one or two groups which you sense will bring hope and positivity into your day and focus your attention on those. While it is wise to limit your time on social media, it is also important to get support, so you may have to work out how you can best achieve this. I would encourage maybe setting a timer so that you aren't on it for too long. Then treat it as if you had done a physical activity and allow yourself to rest after!

Work out what you want from the group and how you will interact. You may decide to simply scroll through the posts and get comfort from things you see there, or you can ask questions, make friends, and get advice, while feeling more understood!

Ironically, I guess the aim is to try and need these groups less and less. The goal is for you to recover from M.E and so it may not always be wise to stay in groups where you are always remembering about your illness. But while you are in recovery, these groups can be a real lifeline and I would highly recommend you investigate some.

I don't use Instagram as much as I do Facebook, but when I was unwell, I did get drawn into following a lot of people who were also unwell. Initially I really enjoyed this as, again, I felt like here were other people I could relate to. People who understood more and didn't think it was a case of being 'just tired'. I ended up following more and more people though and soon, my feed was full of other 'chronic illness warriors'... and very little of people I actually knew. I found that every time I went on Instagram, I was being bombarded with images of illness... and I don't think that did me any good. I would highly recommend you search out a couple of people to follow, but choose people who make you feel good, and don't overload yourself with too many people to follow.

As well as being able to access support groups on social media, you can go down the good old-fashioned route of seeing people in person! It is worth researching whether there are any local M.E. support groups as, although it is obviously exhausting physically seeing people when you are ill, there is nothing quite like actual human contact with someone else. Hopefully, it can be a safe space for you to be able to talk to people going through similar situations and be a safe and positive way of gaining the support you need.

I was very lucky to have the support of the group of people who I did the M.E. course with at The Sanctuary of Healing. When I first went in there, not even willing to accept that I should be there, I felt lost. When I sat through that first session and did a mental tick list of what was being discussed and realised that I actually *should* be there, and I sat with tears streaming down my face, the support I got was invaluable. Although it was hard when I looked around and saw that so many people had been ill for years, sometimes even decades, I knew that I wasn't alone. I wasn't making it up. I wasn't lazy or depressed... I had M.E. I needed to take that seriously and learn about all the things that I could do to help myself. I knew that there was no official cure or treatment, and this was scary, so the support of other people was very much needed.

After the course finished, the group was split into two smaller groups, and we would meet once a week at The Sanctuary and do some more work on our recovery. This was a bit more intense and quite intimate, so I'm glad the group was smaller. We set up a WhatsApp group, so we had that support whenever we needed it. I found this to be so helpful. I loved that we weren't negative throughout this, and we truly did support each other through some difficult experiences. Even though we may not have been in constant contact, just knowing that I had that group of people who wanted to support each other was fantastic. I felt such love from that group as we could all relate to each other. I have made some wonderful friends through it.

I would certainly advise that if you are able to source and attend a support group, that you treat it as a physical activity and make sure you get **plenty** of rest after it. When you are ill, just leaving the house can be a mission in itself. Meeting people can be hard, and all of the emotional aspects of this activity need to be considered. Daft as it may sound, consider it an achievement if you manage to get out to a group, because it truly is! You are doing something amazing for yourself... but be prepared that it can cause additional fatigue, and so it is vital that you treat yourself with compassion and make time out for yourself after. Don't bother about people who don't understand that what they see as a 'simple' act of you getting out the house to attend a group for a couple of hours isn't that big a deal... it really **is**.

I would 100% recommend support groups for anyone going through M.E. as they genuinely can help you feel understood in a way which you may struggle to get anywhere else. One tip I would give is to encourage talk of what people are doing to aid their own recovery and try to ensure that there is positivity within the group (which can sometimes be difficult I know). The aim is come away from the interaction feeling empowered and uplifted, rather than leaving feeling dispirited.

LISTENING TO MYSELF

It may sound simplistic to say that I had to learn how to listen to myself, but I'm pretty sure I won't be the only person who doesn't aways listen to themselves. I was always great at listening to other people's problems/issues and coming up with something which could hopefully help them, but I wasn't always great at listening to **myself** when it came to my own issues.

It's funny how easy it is for us to look at other people and be able to tell what's 'wrong' with them and be able to 'know' what they should do to make their lives better/easier... but it's not always as easy to look inwards at ourselves. We often don't want to do the inner work which is necessary to ensure that we have the best life possible (or we may feel that we don't know where to start). We can be so busy trying to save/fix our loved ones, without taking the time to work on ourselves. We may end up subconsciously looking for distractions from dealing with our own issues, by looking at other people and concentrating on them.

Unfortunately, with an illness such as M.E. there comes a point where you must stop doing that and you must fully concentrate on **you**. This is one of the best things you can do for yourself though, and once you have learned how to do it, it is a vital skill which should be continued for the rest of your life.

When you are ill, you cannot imagine how you may get to a point where you can become grateful for things like pain. When pain and other horrific symptoms are overwhelming in your life, it can be difficult to see that your body is always talking to you and is sending you signals in the hope of keeping you well. When I was really bad and used to read things like this, I used to think it was ridiculous. In fact, it made me quite angry. It may be making you angry too... and I understand that. That's your body talking to you though!! All our emotions and feelings are meant to be *heard*. We try so hard to suppress them because we are taught from an early age not to let out certain feelings. Anger, grief, jealousy and other so called 'negative' emotions should surely be kept inside because to share them would make us look like we are horrible and will make other people uncomfortable. So we are taught not to cry, not to get angry, not to react... but instead to keep it all in. Conversely, we are sometimes even told to downplay other emotions, those of a more 'positive' nature. We shouldn't appear **too** happy, or giddy, or proud of ourselves! Truly, we can't win!

All these emotions end up being supressed, so that we can maintain a happy balance and not upset other people. Just think about what happens when you see someone crying. You, or someone else, may tell them not to cry. You may pass them a tissue (which is a kind gesture I know, *but* it may encourage them to wipe their tears away and stop crying, as opposed to allowing the tears to continue). Boys/men often have an especially tough time with tears, as even today, people may tell them that 'Boys don't cry'. While boys are often brought up to try and mask sadness, girls can be brought up to mask anger. It seems like it's ok for boys to get angry and get in a fight, but quite different when girls do. Of course, I'm just generalising here and know that not everyone feels this way (before the PC brigade take umbrage with me). Society dictates how we share our emotions though, there can be no denying that. Even though there are so many phrases out there telling us things like 'It's good to talk', and 'It's ok to not be ok', there are still so many people who feel that it is shameful to admit to how they are really feeling. So, if we aren't comfortable with expressing our emotions properly and we work hard to keep our true feelings hidden away, what happens to them? Emotions and feelings, like thoughts, are energy. Once they have been created, they don't simply disappear into nothingness. They get trapped inside your body. Hidden away and unable to be released, they can build up. Over time, one feeling adds to another, and another, and another. We probably all know the feeling of reaching our limit and being unable to control ourselves. We can 'blow up' at the slightest thing and wonder why we reacted in such a way when we look back on it. Or we have seen someone act completely out of character for them and wonder what on earth has 'gotten into them'. The truth is, it's usually all of those pent-up emotions which have 'gotten into' them (or us). It's days, weeks, months, years, even decades of keeping a lid on it. Of not letting things be dealt with. Of unsaid words and unexpressed feelings.

Those feelings have energy, and that energy sits inside your body. It can become toxic. Our bodies don't like toxicity, so it sends us signals to say that something is wrong. It may be some pain. It may be a horrible feeling. It may be an unexpected symptom. But because we are busy trying to deal with life, we don't want to deal with anything which may prove to be really difficult, so we ignore those signals. Even when the signals get repeated, we tell ourselves that we will be fine. We make excuses and we look for distractions. We assume that we can get a quick fix in a pill, or we try to numb ourselves through food, alcohol, drugs, exercise, shopping, gambling, or a whole variety of different things which help us to avoid dealing what is going on inside ourselves.

We can only ever cope with so many trapped emotions/feelings before our body does not feel at ease anymore. What is the opposite of not being 'at ease?' Yes, you've guessed it, the body is at 'dis-ease'. You may be able to see where I am going here, and you may not like it. When you are in real physical pain and you have horrific symptoms, with doctors telling you that there is no specific explanation, and other people may have difficulty believing you, and even you can't work out why some days you feel fine and others you feel like you've been hit by a truck – the last thing you may want to hear is that your emotions/feelings are playing a part in your disease/illness. If you are feeling uncomfortable in any way reading this, please take note! Your body is trying to talk to you. It may not feel good... but that does not mean that it is necessarily 'bad'. We often fight against things when we really shouldn't. When I first looked into the mind-body connection I felt like I was somehow being blamed for creating my own illness. I didn't like that. One little bit. Of **course** I didn't want to be ill! Why on earth would ***I*** *create* my own illness?

Especially one as complicated and misunderstood as M.E? It was a preposterous idea! My mind (and body) rejected it. But the more and more research I did, the more I realised there was something in this. The more experts I heard talk about it, the more books I read, podcasts I listened to, the more courses I did and the more work I did on myself... the more I saw that I had a much bigger part to play in my own healing than I had initially thought possible. The more therapies and different sessions I had which helped me deal with things from my past, the more I realised that I had been getting through life while not being fully truthful with myself. I hadn't always spoken my truth. I had been such a people pleaser and helper that I had done things even when I hadn't wanted to. I had felt uncomfortable saying no. I had put myself under so much pressure. I had kept anger in. I had hidden my sadness. I had tried to pretend I was over things which hurt me because society deems that we should be 'over' something by a particular date. I had felt shame for crying. I had allowed myself to be walked all over at times. I had hidden so many emotions for fear of upsetting others. I had even hidden happiness and joy at times because I didn't want to seem inconsiderate when other people weren't as happy as I was. I had suffered from years of feeling guilt for a variety of things and I had never felt like I was good enough. I worried about what people thought of me. I was self-conscious about the way I looked, spoke, and acted. I felt nervous and always tried to cover it up. I had spent years in a mentally difficult job where showing vulnerability was seen as a sign of weakness, and could even put you in danger. I had covered up a whole host of emotions I felt while dealing with traumatic incidents by partaking in the acceptable light heated humour which got you through the toughest times. My body was **full** of pent-up emotions.

Every now and then it would send me signs that I needed to look after myself better. Looking back, I can see a pattern of illness, exhaustion, being run down or just feeling generally horrible... but I chose to ignore that these were signs (well, I guess I didn't really know to be fair) and I just kept going. I may have taken some time off to deal with a particular illness (tonsilitis was one of my body's favourite ways to get my attention when I was particularly stressed and not dealing with things very well), but I would always get back to carrying on, well, carrying on!

After years of ignoring my body, I truly believe that my body had simply had enough. It floored me. It wanted to give me no option but to sit (or even lie) down and do whatever I needed to do to live my best life. I figure it figured that M.E. would do that immediately. But do you know what? It didn't! Not straightaway anyway!

Of course, I could no longer ignore my body. I was ill every single day. I had days where I could hardly move. I got progressively worse... and I believe I would have continued to keep getting worse, if I hadn't done everything I have done in order to change my life. So why didn't I do everything straight away? Why did it take such extreme measures for me to finally slow down enough to truly listen to my body and work out what it wanted so that I could heal myself? Personally, I believe you must be completely ready. You must accept the illness. You have to accept that there is only **you** who can make the changes you need to recover. You must accept that some (or even all) of these changes need to be lifelong. You need to be prepared to commit to yourself. You need to be ok with putting yourself first, even though there may be other people who need you and people who may not understand what you are doing. You need to accept that a 'quick-fix' isn't on its way. You need to be ok with knowing that a 'cure' for M.E. isn't around the corner... indeed (and **please** don't think this is me being pessimistic because I *pray* that my next words are 100% wrong) there may never be a medical cure for it. You need to believe... in YOURSELF.

I will fully admit that it took a long time for me to get to that point. I know there are lots of people out there who will take a lot longer than me to get there, and unfortunately there are people out there who may never get there.

The strange thing is, we get stuck in a certain way of 'being'. We create a comfort zone, and we stay there. Even when that comfort zone is really horrible. It can be hard to pull yourself out of it and into the unknown. People will often say 'My illness isn't me'...but I know that for a while, my illness *was* a huge part of my identity. Even now, my illness is still part of it because my current story is that 'I am in recovery from M.E.' (I do have faith that one day this will change to 'I have recovered from M.E'....and at some point I would love to think that I won't even feel a need to tell people that I had M.E. (unless I am choosing to share about it in order to help someone).

STOPPING THE COMPARISON GAME

I love the phrase 'Comparison is the thief of joy' as I really believe it to be true. I have been caught up in playing the comparison game countless times, and even now I have to make efforts to ensure I don't do it anymore. It can be hard, especially with how we often live our lives through social media. Even without any illness, we can get caught up in watching other people's highlights and assuming that everyone else is living a better life than us somehow. While it's good to see other people happy and we should never feel resentful about their good fortune, there can be no denying that occasionally it can be pretty hard to deal with watching other people live (in our perception) great lives, especially when you don't feel that life is being as good to you.

While that kind of comparison is one thing to deal with for all of us and can be even more difficult when you are ill and you are missing out on so much of what life has to offer, there is also another type of comparison which needs to be stopped.

That is the comparison between who is the most unwell and who has the worst symptoms. I found this to be massively damaging to my emotional health and it affected how I dealt with my everyday life, as well as my recovery.

One thing which is vital for anyone who is ill in any manner, is acceptance of your illness. This is huge and can take some time to come to terms with. Even after an official diagnosis, it can be so difficult to realise that an illness which you have only ever heard about, or known other people with, is suddenly in your own life. It's one thing to hear about someone else having M.E. (or any other illness), and quite another to be diagnosed with it yourself. It can take a lot of work on yourself and support from others to learn how to accept that you are so unwell. It's always helpful to know that you aren't alone, and that other people may have an idea of what you are going through as they are going/have been through it too. I always say that nobody can ever fully know what another person is going through, as we are all individuals and can only ever truly know what we *ourselves* go through. Our thoughts and feelings are our own and cannot ever be exactly the same as anyone else. Even so, it can feel comforting to know that others can empathise with you and have a real awareness of what you are going through.

An issue for me came when I started comparing myself with people who had M.E. and feeling that my symptoms weren't always as bad as theirs, which somehow seemed to invalidate my own illness. While I think it's good to be able to use the phrase 'There's always someone worse off than you' to be able to help you put things into perspective (and I really do think it's important to do this), it's not always good if you are looking at other people who are worse off than you when you aren't in a particularly good way, and make yourself feel that what you are going through isn't as significant. With an illness like M.E. where there are still so many people who unfortunately don't believe in it or don't see it as being overly serious, it can be even harder when you start comparing yourself, as this can potentially lead to you doubting yourself. This was what I sometimes did. I would read about or even speak to people who were more severe than me and it would make me feel like I wasn't that bad. This could then lead to me feeling like I was simply being pathetic or weak, and I would often end up pushing myself. While I was of course glad that my symptoms weren't worse, when I would speak to people who were worse than me, I would feel like I was being petty for complaining/worrying about my own symptoms if they were less severe. This led to me feeling even worse. It's a pretty crazy way of thinking when you look at it properly, but I have no doubt that I am not alone in thinking that way. In fact, I have witnessed it first hand, when I have had people say to me "Oh I shouldn't complain to you though because you are far worse than me." I saw people compare their symptoms or issues to my own and feel that they weren't as validated in their own experiences, which is an awful way to think. Of course, nobody knows what anyone else is truly feeling. Even if you are the most descriptive person in the world, words alone can never show how someone is actually feeling. Everyone is different and feels things differently. One person may get the flu and be absolutely fine, whereas someone else may get really unwell with it. Even with emotions, one person can take something in their stride, while another person may end up having a bit of a break down over it. It's never that one person is stronger than another, or doing something right (or even wrong), it's simply that we all react to things differently. We should not be comparing ourselves to others, unless we are doing it as a way to motivate ourselves to do better in our lives. We can use that comparison to work out how we can improve ourselves, rather than simply wishing that we could do/be better.

Once I realised that me comparing myself in these ways was having a detrimental effect, I knew that I had to stop doing it. I wanted to have the best mental health possible, and this meant that I had to focus on **me**. It's not that I stopped caring about other people (far from it), but I stopped being *as* focused on them, as it was taking me away from dealing with my own feelings. I stopped letting what other people were going through affect me as much personally. I stopped telling myself that I wasn't important, or that my feelings/symptoms weren't valid. I stopped comparing what I was going through to what anyone else was going through. My recovery was never going to be affected by how someone else was, so I had to stop letting other people influence me in a negative way (and it was **me** who was allowing myself to be influenced, as is usually the case if we are honest). There was nobody actually saying to me that because I wasn't as ill as someone else my illness was invalidated; it was all in my own head. Our own minds can be dangerous and can make us feel so much worse when we allow any negativity to be so strong.

In order to stop myself playing this awful comparison game, I had to remove myself from certain situations. I had to be careful on social media. I had joined some online M.E. groups which I realised weren't benefitting me as there was a lot of negativity in them (and please don't think I am saying that these groups aren't beneficial, as some of them are amazing and I am still in some really positive ones which focus on recovery, rather than allowing it to be an open forum for everyone to complain and compare with no hope of any recovery). I had to unfollow a lot of people who I had previously followed from the M.E. world as, while I appreciated that in them sharing their stories which is **so** important in getting awareness and support for M.E., it wasn't helping *me* personally anymore as I was simply comparing my symptoms to theirs. Even with people I had become friends with, I had to stop getting into the comparison conversations, as it wasn't doing me any good. When other people who weren't ill started telling me about someone who they knew with an illness, I would (politely I hope) tell them that this wasn't a helpful conversation for me anymore and that for my own health, I needed to not discuss anything other than something which would offer me hope.

To some people, it can probably seem quite selfish when you say that you are making yourself a priority. However, when you realise that it is neither selfish nor rude to be properly looking after yourself, then things change. It does not mean that you suddenly become an uncaring person. In fact, it can be quite the opposite. When you focus on sorting your own health to the best of your ability, you actually end up with more energy to give to others!

Stopping playing the comparison game really helped me in my recovery and is something that I will strive to always do. The only person I ever want to compare myself to now is *me*. Not in a negative way, only ever in a positive way. I won't compare myself to me thinking about when I was younger, fitter, healthier, slimmer, and then make myself feel bad. I will compare myself and realise how much I have come through and realise how strong I really am. Life is tough, but so am I... and so are you. It is always good to be proud of your own achievements, and that is difficult to do if you get stuck in comparison. Stay in your own lane, work on yourself, and let everyone else deal with their own issues.

WORKING ON MYSELF

I will never stop working on **me**. I believe that we can always keep learning, keep growing, keep moving on. We can always improve our health and our happiness. I don't believe that we should dwell on our past, but we should learn lessons from it and use them to forge how we want our present, and our future to be. When I was really ill, I used to look towards the future and plan how I would be when I was 'better'. At some point though, I realised that I had to focus on how I was **now**. Having a goal which keeps you going is amazing and will help to keep you motivated, but I had to realise that I didn't always want to be waiting to be a certain way before I would consider myself as being happy or being recovered. I wanted to be happy each day, no matter how I was feeling.

I consider myself to be an eternal student. I tell my own children that even though I am no longer in school, I am always still learning. I learn from other people; I learn from situations I am in myself and I learn from seeing what others go through. It is all important. I choose to fill my mind with things which keep me learning every single day. I hope that this never stops. I don't think that there will ever come a time where I think I know everything...or even know so much that I would consider myself such an expert that I no longer need to learn anything more.

Life is always changing... and so must we. When I did my degree in Food and Nutrition a few years ago (ok, ok, it was a lot more than a few years ago, I just like to kid myself that it wasn't), I was taught things that have since turned out to be wrong. All the things I have learned about food during my recovery makes me realise that even the 'experts' don't know everything. Decades ago, doctors were promoting cigarettes. Nowadays, it would be impossible to think of a doctor recommending a particular brand of cigarette for someone with asthma! While I fully appreciate that right now, people may question things like the removal of processed foods and sugar from my own diet, I am confident that in the future, this will be far more normal for a lot more people and we will be horrified by the diets we ate for so long, just as so many of us are horrified at the thought of smoking now.

The world has changed so much and will continue to do so. Our priorities have changed and we now value things which once would have seemed crazy to us. People wear exhaustion and how busy they are like a badge of honour. It's like the busier you are seen to be, the more important you must be. In some ways we have more time available for ourselves than we had a century ago and we have far more time saving devices. Yet we live in a society where we don't ever seem to have time for ourselves. So many of us believe that time spent on ourselves is selfish. We believe that we should always be 'doing', rather than just 'being'. I believe it is so important to keep learning about myself so that I continue to make the right choices for me. I don't ever want to get caught up in being so busy that I fail to look after myself properly. I want to learn how to be the best role model for my own children...

and I want to be able to learn about things so that I can help other people by coming from an informed perspective.

I plan on always keeping my mind positive. I accept that I will have bad days. With or without M.E. we all have 'bad' days. At the time of writing this section I have a really horrible ear infection. It's been hard to deal with. I know it's a reminder to look after myself properly and when I've looked back, I've realised that I have let some things slide. I got a bit caught up in a couple of things which made me make myself less of a priority. I know better! It's been hard as both of my children have been really upset! They hear 'infection' and they panic as they know that I started with M.E. following a chest infection. They both told me that they were worried that I would get really ill again. Sadly, Jack still holds some fear that I may die. This illness changes lives and anybody who believes that it is 'tiredness' or that it is not really that serious are very much mistaken. I have learnt so much about this illness, but even more about myself along this journey, that I never want to forget about it all. I completely understand anyone who, when they recover from M.E. never want to talk about it again. The fear of relapse is strong and real. For me though, I truly believe that helping others understand more about this illness and encouraging others to go on their own journeys of self-discovery, will be an important part of my life. I plan to keep learning more about myself and to find out ways in which I can continue to help others (while always being conscious of keeping my own energy safe in a way I didn't always do before and during my illness). I will continue to read wonderful books, listen to amazing podcasts, go on fantastic courses, meditate, work on my inner self, and grow as an individual. I hope to learn new skills and continue to be proud of myself for all the work I do.

Learning is never just for children. You don't have to go back to school to learn. You don't have to spend loads of money to learn new skills. You simply have to be open to creating the best life possible for yourself. You truly deserve the best in life and keeping on learning about yourself is one way you can get that! It is certainly what I plan to do.

EXTRAS

As well as everything I have written about which I feel have been the most important things for my own recovery, there have been a few other things which I feel have helped me along my recovery journey so I thought I would share them briefly here, as I would certainly recommend giving them a try.

Magnesium baths/spray

Magnesium is a mineral which plays an important role in the body. It can help support muscle and nerve function, and affects energy production. It can reduce stress and even help you sleep for longer. Every cell in your body can use magnesium to function and it can help with the biochemical reactions performed by enzymes. Nowadays, there are several reasons why we may be deficient of a good amount of magnesium in our diets and so it is certainly worth considering taking a supplement of it, especially if you have M.E.

Since magnesium plays such an important part in energy production, it is worthwhile getting your doctor to check your magnesium levels. It helps in the reaction which causes ATP (Adenosine triphosphate... don't panic, I'm not going to turn this into a science lesson, but it is important). ATP is the main source of energy in our cells. For it to be active, it must bind to a magnesium ion! So you can see how vital magnesium is for our cellular energy!

As well as a supplement though, magnesium can be absorbed through your skin. I use magnesium salts in my bath and try to make sure I have at least one bath a week with them in.

When I suffered with a lot of pain, I would also use a magnesium spray on some of the affected areas and found this useful. You do have to be careful not to use too much. The spray especially can sting a bit at first if you are not used to it... and you certainly don't want to be using it all the time but used sparingly, it can make a difference!

Reducing toxic chemicals

When you look at how many products we come into contact with every day which have numerous chemicals in them, it is no wonder that our systems may become overloaded with things which aren't very good for us. From the foods we eat, to the products we use on our skin and hair, to the cleaning products we use around the house, we have never been exposed to more man-made chemicals. Of course, we all want to have clean bodies, clothes, houses, and cars... but there is certainly a big possibility that we may be causing harm to ourselves with what we are using and consuming on a daily basis. When I did research on this, I couldn't believe that I hadn't thought about this earlier. However, even though it makes total sense to me to cut down on chemicals, it is something I have struggled with! I love a clean house, and a clean body of course! I love strongly scented products and even love the smell of bleach (it makes me think things are clean, and I love that!) so when I had to think about trying to reduce some things, I didn't want to let go! I know it may sound silly, but it felt like yet something else I was going to have to give up and change, and I didn't particularly want to! But of course, as with everything else, I had to look at whether I wanted wellness, or illness. It's much easier when I think of it like that.

I spent some time looking into some more friendly, toxic free products and made some changes. I started making some of my own products using essential oils and was fairly pleased with the results. I haven't gone as strict with this as with some of the other things I have discussed, but I do think it is worth looking into this and considering making some changes. As with other things it can end up being more expensive and take more time when you make your own products... but if there is a chance it can help with your wellness, then it is always worth it. Of course, you will be doing yourself more good and there can certainly be no harm in your reducing the toxicity you are subjecting yourself to!

Cold Showers

When you get ill, lots of people will give you a lot of advice, whether you ask for it or not. People genuinely want to try and help and while it can sometimes be difficult to hear people recommend that if you just 'think positively' or try meditating then you will get better, remember that you may also get some good advice and recommendations along the way. One thing you could try is having a place to write down any books/podcasts/films/methods etc which people recommend to you, and then you can choose to spend some time exploring them at a time which feels right for you. I was told about a few things along the way which I didn't act upon straightaway, but when I looked later, they were helpful. You just have to be ready.

One recommendation I received was from a lovely friend who mentioned that I should investigate the Wim Hof method/story. I had a quick look and saw it was about concentrating on your breathing and jumping into cold lakes, neither of which particularly appealed to me at the time, so I didn't take it any further. A while later, I came across this again, but still wasn't interested. When it came up for the third time, I decided to see what all the fuss was about. I'm so glad I did.

Wim Hof has an incredible story, and I would certainly encourage you to check it out. I won't go into his story here but will say that he is able to push his body to incredible extremes and believes that anyone is capable of doing the same with the correct training, and of course, the right mindset.

He recommended, along with lots of other people doing the same, cold showers and focusing on your breathing to help optimise your body.

I didn't fancy it at first! When your body is racked with pain, the last thing you want to do is choose to inflict more hardness on yourself, so the thought of having a cold shower every day did *not* go down well. The more I researched it though, the more it made sense to me. When I had started feeling somewhat better, I decided to give it a go. I found some of his breathing techniques online and started doing them and I really enjoyed them. In fact, I think they are a good way to get into meditation, as you are really focusing in on your breathing which is an effective way to try and clear your mind a bit. I then worked up to having a cold shower. It was hard. I didn't want to do it. The funny thing is, I *still* don't really want to do it... and at the time of writing this, I have been doing it every day for over 18 months! It's quite amusing really as I have this little argument with myself every morning in the shower. The conversation will go something like this..." I don't want to do this. You never want to do it. Yeah, but today I **really** don't want to do it. I know, you said that yesterday, and the day before. I know, but today is different. Erm, so is every day. I don't want to be cold today though, and it's not nice. Yeah, but once you've done it you actually quite enjoy it and you know it can make you feel better. I know, I know, I just don't fancy it today, I don't feel up to it. Tough s**t, you're doing it!" At this point, I will reach forward and turn the shower to cold! I will take a huge deep breath and brace myself for the cold to hit. Sometimes I wince, other times I don't, I often swear! Then I manage to relax into it. I focus on my breathing, and I start to quite enjoy it! I quite often put a song on. 'Fight Song' on and 'Lovely day' are two of my favourites for this. I like to have a bit of a power dance while I'm allowing the cold water to work its magic.

There are lots of benefits to cold water showers or even cold-water swimming. I have now started to do the cold water/wild swimming and it feels amazing. Obviously, I wouldn't like to recommend this for people who are still actively very unwell, and would recommend that anyone thinking of giving it a go to make sure that they seek out someone to swim with who is knowledgeable about cold water swimming as it can be dangerous (and obviously **never** to swim alone). It certainly wakes you up and makes you feel alive, which is a great start. It improves your circulation, can relieve muscle pain, can calm inflammation and pain, and can even give you better skin and hair (OK, I appreciate that in the bid to beat M.E. this may not be particularly high on the agenda, but then again, I don't think anyone will ever complain at looking that little bit brighter as it can definitely help to boost our mood, which has its own benefits of course!).

As with so many of the things I have done/ do to help improve my health, mindset helps a lot with this one. I know that having a cold shower makes me feel better, so even though I don't always especially feel like doing it, I do it anyway.

PART 3

WHERE I AM NOW

Currently, my life is pretty amazing. I have never been more grateful for life and appreciative of so many things. It's brilliant when each day I can be so thankful for things I used to take for granted. The simple act of waking up and realising that I'm no longer in horrific pain is fantastic. To be able to get out of bed unaided is a dream. To know that my children don't worry each day that I may be dying is incredible.

When I used to read other people's recovery stories and they said that they were now grateful for their illness because it had taught them so much about themselves and had ended up making them feel like they were better people now, I used to swear at them! I used to think that there was no way I could **ever** be grateful for feeling like this... even though I dreamed that one day I may be able to say the same. Well, I'm happy to say that now I **can (**and regularly do) say that.

There may (or there may not – I'm hopeful!) always be some emotion attached to thoughts of my illness and I may feel sad that my beautiful family had to suffer along with me during that time, but I also know that it has made all of us stronger in the end.

Being able to talk about it fully (with each other and with professionals) has helped us all as a family and we will continue to do that whenever we feel the need to, as we have all realised the importance of doing that, rather than keep bottling things up.

At the time of writing this book, I feel great. My first Christmas during recovery was tiring... but we did a lot! We did more than we would usually do at Christmas, and we all felt tired out, although obviously it affected me more. Not long after Christmas, I got Covid. This had been a real concern for us during the pandemic. James had been convinced at the start of it that if I got Covid, I would probably die. He did not think my body was in any way strong enough to deal with it. That was so awful to hear when he told me that. Thankfully when I did eventually get it, I didn't fare too badly. All four of us got it the same week so our isolation period was just one length of time, which we didn't mind at all. I did get poorly, but nowhere near what I had once worried about. In comparison to what I had been through, it wasn't that bad. In fact, it wasn't even as bad as one of my 'good' days when I was in a really bad state! I think the hardest thing in one way was the fact that we were all at home again and so I felt concerned about putting my brave face on. Jack especially got worried again that I may die, which was hard. But I reassured him that I would be fine and reiterated every time I needed to rest, that I was ok. If anything, I'm sure I recovered much faster because I was being so careful to make sure that I was properly looking after myself. When I felt tired, I rested. Immediately! I kept up with all the healing things that I had been doing (other than leaving the house of course... I was once again very grateful for a garden and thankful for lovely friends who took Chewy for a daily walk) and so I know that I was keeping myself healthy. Strangely, I noticed that when I had Covid, I had a lot more cravings for unhealthy foods! I knew it was old habits kicking back in (or trying to) as well as a general lack of energy, which meant that I just wanted to grab quick and easy food!

At the time of writing this, I am working at The Sanctuary of Healing café. I love The Sanctuary and so many times when I was there for treatments and courses, I would call it my second home. I would feel such peace and calmness taking over me every time I went in, and I remember saying that I would absolutely love to work there one day.

I saw an advertisement to work in the cafe four days a week one day when I was about seven months into my recovery. I remember wishing that I felt strong enough to do that but not feeling I could. I must have put something out into the universe because a few days later I saw an advert asking for someone to work two days a week! I knew that this was the sign I had been waiting for. The old me would have hesitated and put off enquiring and would have been filled with self-doubt that I could do it. The new me knew to give it a go! The very next week, I started my new job and I absolutely love it!

Having always worked, I had missed working so much when I was unwell. I always knew that I wanted to get back to work... but I also accepted that it would need to be something which would support my recovery. Thankfully I have found that, and I work with the best and most supportive team ever.

I currently work two days a week, very occasionally more. At first when I started working again, I was going to aim to get back to full time work as soon as possible! I believed that working full time would **prove** that I had fully recovered. I soon realised that this was the wrong way to go about it though. While it's important to have goals to aim for, I know that I must be careful to not overdo things again... and certainly not to 'prove' that I'm better. I don't have to prove anything to anyone... not even myself. If I did feel a need to prove myself, then the proof is in the fact that each day I wake up feeling so good!

My job is lovely. I haven't worked in hospitality since I left university and I wasn't sure how I would manage... but I absolutely love it! I work with amazing people, in one of my favourite places and get to meet lovely customers every day! It was a bit of a shock to the system being on my feet again all day, but thankfully it didn't take too long to get used to it. I know that I am very lucky because everyone at The Sanctuary knows my story, because they have walked it with me. We have so many people coming in for healing, wellbeing treatments and meditations and I love being able to talk to like-minded people. I like to share my story with people who come in with M.E. or similar illnesses, as I love to be able to show people that you **can** get better. It isn't easy of course, but I think that everyone should have faith in themselves that they can improve. People often get a shock when I tell them that I am in recovery from M.E. as I genuinely believe that you would not be able to tell. I know it's annoying when people say, "Oh you don't look ill" and I experienced this many times when I was ill. What I have found now is that some people who have M.E. now look at me and say, "Well you can't have been **that** ill." I remember being really upset the first time someone said this to me but now I know that it is no reflection on me, rather it is a reflection on the person thinking/saying that. I don't mean that to sound rude in any way... because I have unfortunately thought that myself in the past about other people. I remember hearing about people who had recovered and without knowing the full story, I would assume that the person must not have been as ill as I was. It's a hard thing to stop doing, but when you stop comparing and judging others, things become easier. I realised that me thinking thoughts like this were a way of me justifying why others could get better, but that I probably wouldn't. I know lots of people will think that the more unwell you are, or the longer you have had the illness, the less likely you are to ever recover... but I truly do believe that **anyone** can recover. There are enough stories out there showing that this is the case. Once you can get good control over your mindset, *believe* that you can get better and put the *work* in to getting better, anything is possible.

I have been able to start volunteering again which makes me super happy. I initially went back to my old school listening to readers, which I loved, as I have a real passion for encouraging children to have a love of reading. I was also able to step in and help at Cubs whenever I was needed. I am now volunteering at my children's school in different ways. Doing these things make me feel really fulfilled. Volunteering feels good for my soul, and I hope that I am always able to do this in some way as it is so important to me. I am careful though to make sure that my energy is protected, and that it works around my family life. While I love giving my time to others for important things like this, I never want to be at a point where it is putting me in a position where I am overwhelmed. I have had to learn how to say no, and I accept that sometimes this will mean I am unable to do things, even if I want to. But for now, everything is working out nicely and I am so grateful that I am able to do it.

I can exercise again! Oh, how I missed being able to go running and walking. It feels incredible to be able to do that again. I do have to catch myself sometimes as I can feel my old personality traits slipping in and I feel I want to push myself. While I think it's good to want to do more, I also am very aware that pushing my body too much will not work for me. I must listen *very* hard to my body. Even though my mind may be whispering and enticing me to 'just do that extra bit', when my body whispers that I shouldn't, I *always* listen to my body. Genuinely, that can be difficult to do... but I know it's always the **right** thing to do. I never want to end up back in a position where I can't walk again and so I'm very much one step at a time now. The good thing is that I now feel I have a healthier relationship with exercise. I used to exercise to stay slim and so that I could stuff my face with as much junk food as I wanted. Of course, I wanted to stay healthy, but I guess it wasn't as important. Now I don't have the body hang ups I used to, plus I'm not eating junk food anymore, so staying slim isn't a concern of mine. I used to run for peace of mind, and while I still do this, I have also learned to get that feeling through meditation and mindfulness. I have peace of mind so much more now. I don't need to push my body and I feel much happier about that. During the editing of this book, I have just enjoyed my first ever ski holiday! I'm not going to lie - learning to ski in your forties is hard... really hard! The main thing I have taken from it is that **mindset truly is everything**! I have not had to have so many 'words' with myself since the start of my recovery as I had to during that holiday! Ultimately, I cannot quite believe I am now able to be physically or mentally able to do such an activity, and my gratitude for it has been immense (although my ski instructor got a shock when he got shouted at for attempting to tell me to "Push through the pain").

I am the mum I wanted to be. I can do things with my children again which I haven't been able to over the last few years, and that feels incredible. I feel like I am a better mum now because I have learned so much about myself and I feel blessed to share this with my children. All of the mindset work I have done, and continue to do on a daily basis, is wonderful and I love being in a position where I can teach the kids to work on their own mindsets too. I want to be a positive role model to my children, and I genuinely feel that my children have already learned so much which will help them as they transition into young adults. Of course, I may feel sad about what they have gone through in having such an unwell mum, but I choose not to dwell on that. I know that there have been a lot of positives too for them; they have certainly learned a lot of life skills and they are both capable in jobs around the house! They also have great empathy and certainly understand that illness is not always visible. They have seen first-hand that people **can** recover from illness and that when you put your mind to something you truly want, and put the work into it, you can achieve it. I hope that this gives them strength and resilience in the future. We talk a lot more now and are open about what is going on. I guess that as the teenage years hit, I may lose some of that, but I'm hoping that by setting these foundations, we will do well. I hope that I have shown my children that it is ok to ask for, and accept, help, because I really believe that so many people would benefit from doing this more! I want them to see that it is good to love yourself, to be grateful for your health, and realise that prioritising their own self-care is never selfish. Self-care is **never** self-indulgence – its is actually self-preservation.

I am a loved and loving wife. My marriage is incredibly important to me, and I am so glad that not only have James and I got through the past few years, but we have also actually gotten stronger. When I got diagnosed with M.E., I told James that I would totally understand if he wanted to leave me. Of course, he was upset that I would even suggest this... but I know that for some relationships, having a serious illness can tear you apart. I know that some of my friendships weren't strong enough to last the course of my illness, and I do understand it. When your life changes so much, it can be hard for other people. Their lives change too, and they may no longer find themselves being compatible with you. I didn't want James to stay with me out of a sense of duty and so I would sometimes tell him (especially on my darker days) that it was fine if he left me. Of course, the last thing I wanted was for him to leave me. But I loved him so much that I didn't want to be ruining his life (which was sometimes how I thought). James always had faith in me. He saw things in me which I couldn't and so he always assured me that I would one day recover. I'm so glad he was right.

It was so hard for him with everything he went through, and I will be eternally grateful for him.

I can say **no** to things which I don't want to do... and I can say **yes** when people offer help! Both things are *so* important. They are important for everyone of course, but especially for people who have health issues. As humans, we aren't meant to go it alone. That doesn't mean that you have to be married/live with someone, or even have children. What it does mean is that we are supposed to have people in our lives who we can get support from. It's a give and take thing though. I learned that I couldn't keep giving and giving, without ever taking. That can be difficult when giving seems to be part of your nature. Once I realised that it was more than ok to say no to protect my own energy, I became much happier. It is never nice to experience the feeling of being taken advantage of and I do my best to make sure this doesn't happen now. Unfortunately, when you get used to always saying yes to others, even to the detriment of your own health, you may sometimes find that you start to begrudge doing certain things. This is no way to live. Giving should feel good. If it doesn't, then you shouldn't really be doing it. Of course, there will be times where you *do* have to do things you don't always want to... but these times shouldn't be taking you over. You should be able to find peace and joy in what you are doing. I am very conscious now of what I commit to. I am very open about it too as I think that helps people understand and makes me feel better. If there is something I know is too much for me, for any reason, I will simply say that I won't do it because I need to watch my energy. People who know my story (hopefully) understand straightaway. For anyone who doesn't know my story and may think it is a strange thing to say, well I don't worry about that! In fact, I hope that me saying this may act as a prompt for them to think about whether they are protecting their own energy!

I get out of my house every single day. I will never take for granted how amazing it is simply to have the strength to be able to do this. It helps having a dog, as I get to take him out every day; but even without him, I would still do this. Come rain, shine, snow, or hail, I get myself outside. Even if it is only to be outside in my own garden, it is so important for me to do that! I appreciate everything about being outside and love to be in nature.

I do the school run and take the children to their activities without it being an issue. This is genuinely a big thing for me. There were days when I would save up all my energy just so that I could do one school run... and it would totally exhaust me. Of course, there were also days when I couldn't manage even one school run. I hated those days as I felt like such a failure. I had to learn that accepting help with these things was completely necessary, but it still hurt me that I couldn't do something as seemingly simple as this. I remember recently being in the car and both kids were arguing, and I felt stressed about it. Then suddenly, I thought "This is wonderful!" I told myself that I had wanted to feel as 'normal' as possible... and here it was! Driving a car, running a bit late and listening to my kids shouting at each other! How fabulous that this level of 'normality' had returned! It really helped to calm my stress levels, that's for sure.

I can do housework with no issues! It may seem silly that I add this in as an achievement but believe me, it really is. I love that I can clean and tidy my own house again without worrying that it will put me in bed for a week! However, I do feel it important to add here that this is one area I do accept help with! I love a clean house and I used to spend a lot of time and energy cleaning (pre-M.E.). I'm a big believer in 'tidy house, tidy mind' (although that doesn't always translate to my car, much to James' disgust) and I really struggle when my house is a mess. I must admit that I have accepted that my house doesn't **have** to be as clean as I used to like it, and I am far better than I used to be in being ok about things being a bit of a mess. Although I have always quite enjoyed cleaning, I now know that there are other things I would rather be doing with my time. So, while I do still enjoy giving the house a good blitz, or even just keeping on top of it, I am not prepared to give it the same level of my time and energy as I used to. However, I still want a clean and tidy house! So, I must accept help! The kids got involved in housework even before I was ill. Obviously, they helped a lot more when I was ill - and they still help now. They have their set jobs, and they do those, as well as helping with other things as and when needed. We will also have times where we clean and tidy together as a family. Daft as it may sound, I absolutely love this! We blast some music on, and we will spend an hour at a weekend where we all pitch in and help do the house! It feels great doing it, and especially great when it's all done! I have stopped thinking that everything must be done **my** way (ok, I would still **like** everything done my way, I mean my way is *surely* the most logical, but I've got better at letting things go) I realised that I can't complain at the kids if they don't keep their rooms tidy all the time. It's actually **me** who wants their rooms to be tidy! So, if I want them to be as tidy as I would like them to be, I need to be ok with doing it myself. **Or** I accept that they are ok with how their rooms are and leave well enough alone! They soon realise that when they can't find something that they need to get cracking with tidying!

We also have an amazing cleaner. We sorted this when I was really ill, and I felt horrific about it. It felt like I was handing over control of something important for some reason. I felt like a failure. It's crazy because now I look at it in a completely different way! My wonderful cleaner is a professional at her job, and I pay to have a service done! Just like I pay the window cleaners, or the milk man, or someone to clean the car. I know how lucky I am to be able to afford to have this help. I felt awful initially however having someone come into my home to do something which not only had I always been capable of doing but had also enjoyed; I felt like I was giving away another part of me. Thankfully, I don't see it like that now. That time where someone is there to help do chores for me, means that I have more time and energy to spend on myself, and on my family. I am glad that I feel ok to do this now.

I can go shopping again... as in physically going to a shop. I love that I can do this. I became so dependent on internet shopping when I was ill, and it was a real lifeline for me. I like internet shopping for many reasons and will always continue to do it where necessary. It's great for time and energy saving, whether you are unwell or not. But I did miss going out to an actual shop. It is something I will never take for granted again. It feels so good to be able to go to a shop and not have to wonder whether I will be able to physically walk around the shop, whether I have the strength to carry a basket or push a trolley, and wondering whether, even if I can do that, will I then be able to make it home? The whole sensory experiences involved with shopping that I never used to even be aware of, such as bright store lighting (or just natural light), the fact that other people are there, having to interact with other people and the noise level, are no longer an issue for me. It is amazing when you break things down, how much we *truly* do have to be grateful for in our lives and I like to remind myself of this as often as I can. Even though I don't go out to shop massively in actual shops, I am always very appreciative whenever I manage to do it. A bit like when you have young children and 'nipping' to the shop becomes a thing of the past, so it did with having M.E. I love that sometimes I don't even think twice about it until I'm back in the car... and then I remember and take a couple of minutes to feel thankful for where I am at.

I am now able to watch a bit more TV. I choose to stick with not watching a lot as I do know that certain things may end up triggering me and I don't see the point in putting myself in that position. I still choose to watch mainly positive things. I have no issue with this as I really have changed my mindset about it. I love my life and I don't see any reason why I would want to numb my brain with what I now see as mindless TV, which never leaves me feeling good after watching it. I do feel more comfortable now though with watching more with the kids and a bit more with James. To be honest, it's had a good effect on all of us as we love watching things like documentaries together now.

I see more of my friends. Seeing friends when you are so ill can be hard. It is unfortunately quite often exhausting. I had to accept that if I saw friends (where I would usually try my best to put on a brave face so they wouldn't know just how bad I was), it would potentially have a huge impact on my home life, and I would feel guilty that I was taking away from my family. It's a hard balance, as it's important to still see friends but it's vital that you put your health and energy first. I would now advise others, and myself, to have the courage to be truthful with friends. When you are tired, *say* that you are tired. Good friends will always understand. And those who don't... well, you already know the truth of that! While I haven't returned to the social life I used to have, I'm actually ok with it. I make the effort to see the people I want to and I am happy with that. I'm not quite as good in groups as I used to be and I prefer to spend quality time with the people I choose to have in my life. I have forged stronger connections with certain people who are more like-minded and prefer to cultivate these relationships. I guess it is harder when you have become different in a lot of ways. I don't usually drink anymore, I don't eat the same and my mindset has changed so much. I know that I'm not the same person I used to be, and while I'm more than happy with who I am now, I appreciate that's not for everyone. Being true to myself is so important now... and when I've had enough of anything, I have no qualms in leaving, rather than pushing myself! I still love people, before you think I've turned into a grouch! I just prefer to choose to be around people who bring joy to my life.

I go out without worrying that I will get quickly exhausted. I no longer get anxious that I may suddenly be unable to walk, or lose the ability to talk, or be overcome with such horrific pain that I want to just crumple up into a ball and cry. I enjoy my time out without thinking in the back of my mind that I know I am going to pay for this. I can enjoy life. And boy, do I enjoy life! I have genuinely never enjoyed life so much. I truly know that every single day is a gift. Even if I have days where I know I need to take it easy, I am thankful to be so in tune with my body that I can realise this and choose to act accordingly.

I have become more relaxed around food. While I still eat very carefully, and always will, I am not as strict as I was in those first six months of healing. I believe that by being so careful initially, I gave my body the best chance of healing and I know that what I put into my body makes a huge difference to me (as it does to all of us). However, I know that there are times when I will choose to eat outside of my regular diet. When this is the case, I ensure I never beat myself up for it. I really believe that if you have negative emotions around the food you eat, then you will not be doing your body any good. If I have a sugary product, some bread or a glass of wine now, I make a conscious decision to enjoy it, rather than living in fear of what it may do to my body. In all honesty, this is something I have had to work particularly hard on, as I realised that I had a lot of fear around the foods I was consuming for a while. I will never choose to go back to the way I used to eat... but I also won't mentally punish myself for eating a little differently every now and then.

I called this book 'Finding Me From M.E.' for a reason. I truly believe that having this illness has helped me to find the **real** me. It has set me off on a path of learning to be happy with who I am. To be fine with doing the things I want to do without always feeling the need to put other people first. I make myself a priority. I choose to practice self-care and feel that I am a far better role model to my children than I was when I was running around after everyone else and not getting full enjoyment out of my own life. I now love myself. Which sounds strange to say and I know that some people will think that it's a big-headed thing to say, but it is definitely not.

Every day I am so grateful for my life. I can find gratitude in the most random things and find that I am able to discover positives in pretty much any negative situation! That's not to say that I no longer have any struggles! With the best will in the world, life will always present me with struggles, but I now know how to deal with things better. I don't bury my head in the sand and suppress my feelings when things go wrong. I deal with things as and when they happen, so I don't spend unnecessary time and energy overthinking things. I accept that when things are not in my control, it doesn't do me any good worrying about them and so I find ways to quieten my mind and move on. I have become more spiritual (note... this does not mean I am more religious – that is a totally different thing). I know that when I get stuck in unhelpful (negative) thinking, I am allowing unwanted things into my life. When I focus on the good that I have in my life, then more good things happen for me. I am a big believer in the law of attraction. While it may sound simplistic in some ways, it definitely isn't always simple. We have been conditioned to think certain ways, even if we do not realise it. We hold ourselves back with our own limiting beliefs, so even if we think we want something, we are quite often blocking ourselves from getting it.

I feel I could write for hours about mindset. Whenever anyone asks me what the biggest change I have made in my recovery journey, or the best tip to heal, I will **always** say doing mindset work! Without doubt, it has been my greatest weapon in the 'fight' to get better. If I hadn't had the right mindset, I would not have been able to commit fully to myself. I would not have been able to make the dietary changes, or learn to rest properly, or to always pace myself regardless of how I was feeling that day or to get myself outside each day no matter what the weather was doing or to stick with daily meditation even when I was busy or unsure whether it was doing anything. I would not have had the strength to say no to things I didn't want to do (or didn't feel up to doing), or indeed the strength to say yes to offers of help. I would not have had the courage to ask for support when I needed it. I would not have started gentle but purposeful movement and built it up in a way that was right for my body, without pushing myself because I felt like I 'should' be able to do more. I would not have stuck with my decision to make changes such as not watching TV, even when it felt like I was being overly cautious for not watching a programme. I would not have been brave enough to admit that I needed professional help from a counsellor because I was struggling to come to terms with the seriousness of the illness. I would not have fought feeling silly standing in front of a mirror and telling myself positive affirmations in an attempt to feel better about myself. I would have struggled to accept that I could take more control over the medication I was taking. I would have possibly given into the illness, and potentially given up. I may have accepted that my illness would be here to stay forever and there was nothing I could do about it, other than wait for a miracle cure or keep throwing money at different treatments in the hope that one would eventually prove to be a 'quick fix'. I would not have done all the *work* which I **needed** to do to help myself heal.

All the changes I have made in my life have made my life amazing. Some of them have been more difficult than others. Some may prove to be a challenge forever, but I accept that, because I never want to go back to how I was when I was really unwell. When I started writing this book, I was unsure as to whether I would always class myself as being 'in recovery from M.E.' or would be confident enough to say that I have fully recovered from M.E. However, I'm delighted to say that I believe that I *am* recovered, and I truly do have confidence that I will never be *that* ill again. This may mean that I will always have to pace myself in certain ways, but I am absolutely fine with that. It most probably means that I will never go back to my old habits of eating, and again, I'm fine with that. It will mean that I will **always** have to listen to my body, and I certainly know that this will only ever benefit me. It means that I will get used to some people thinking I'm a little bit strange when I don't eat the cake, have a celebratory alcoholic drink, don't watch the latest drama on TV, go home when I'm tired no matter what time it is, or when I say no to helping out with something I would have done without question in the past. If all these things mean that I will stay well, then I'm in for the long haul! There is literally nothing that I have done in my recovery journey which can have a detrimental effect on me. Everything I have done has only bettered my health and so I really feel I would be foolish to return to my old habits, which were never helpful for me in the first place.

People may (and do) ask where I get my pleasure from if I choose to not eat chocolate or join them in a drink, and my answer is simple and clear (albeit fairly long I realised after I wrote it). I get my pleasure from **life**. I get my pleasure from waking up everyday pain and symptom free. I enjoy appreciating so much about my amazing life. I get my pleasure from all the wonderful things which I used to take for granted. I am happy knowing that I have taken back control of my own life so that now my children and husband don't have to be concerned about whether I am dying. I take pleasure from having a mind which is clearer than it has ever been. I take pleasure in the fact that I no longer allow things which are out of my control to plague me with worry. I love having faith that whatever happens in my life is meant to be. I may not *like* everything which occurs in my life, and I know that there will always be challenging times ahead, but I know that everything in life is an experience... and that there is nothing I can't get through. People may think this is a naïve way to think...but it serves me well. Life is full of choices. It is full of what people perceive to be 'good' and 'bad'. I choose to focus on the 'good' and trust that things will always work out for me, one way or another.

My illness could have beaten me. I am not cocky enough to say that I have beaten 'it', because I am only too aware that if I don't continue living a healthy life where I ensure that I am always taking care of myself properly, I could end up back at square one. Having M.E. has taught me that life is so precious. I had to get to grips with what I believe made me ill. Not everyone will like to hear this, but I believe for me personally, I got ill for a reason. Without me turning inwards and doing the work on myself, I am not sure I would have ever got better. Changing my diet and being outside each day has worked wonders... but it is the inner work and mindset work which has been vital. It has been about dealing with emotions; it has been about sorting through past traumas and learning to let them go; it's been about discovering the true me and becoming happy with her.

One thing which is necessary for anyone who is unwell and wants to get better, is to sit down and be truthful with yourself. How much do you want to get better? Before you get annoyed at that question and dismiss me because of *course* everyone wants to get better, ask yourself how much do you *really* want it? As in... what are you prepared to **do**, and to **not** do, in order to get yourself better? How much *responsibility* will you take in your own healing? As we know, M.E. is an illness that, as yet, has no medical cure and no 'official' treatment. You could be fooled into thinking that if you have M.E. you are likely to never recover. But you **can** recover. You truly can! It may take a lot longer than you would like, and you may have to accept that you may have life changing experiences along the way. It may temporarily cost you your job, your social life, some relationships, and part of who you are in this journey... but I 100% believe that anyone with this illness can get better. It will usually be a case of trial and error. There is **no** quick fix. What works for one person may not work for you. Something may work for you for a while, but then maybe not forever. It is very frustrating, and you may feel like it is pointless to keep 'battling' on. The point isn't to keep fighting though, it is far better to make peace with your body; treat it with love, listen to it and work out what it needs. This may take a long time, to be able to listen to your body and know what the symptoms are trying to tell you. However, when you put the work in to yourself and persevere, then it will come. I was once convinced that I couldn't do a lot of the things I do now, so I can understand how difficult it is.

A friend asked me recently how long I was going to keep up my new way of eating. I replied 'forever'. She told me that she didn't think she could do that herself. I understood why she may think that. I told her that I don't think about it as being forever (unless someone asks me a question like that), I think if it as one day at a time. For me, it's a simple thing. I either choose to stay well... or I choose to accept that I may be ill again. For whatever reason, my body has decided that if I don't listen to it, I will have horrific symptoms. So to not listen to it would be foolish. My body doesn't work in the same way as someone without M.E. At one time I would have been so angry about that (and trust me, I have done a lot of grieving over it and had to work through that) but now I think differently. I feel grateful that my body wants to keep me protected. I know that my 'soul'/inner energy wasn't always happy playing the parts I used to play, always looking after everyone else above myself. Now I know that I must keep that part of me happy, otherwise I could end up ill again. Whether I think this is fair or not doesn't matter, because this is just the way it is.

Nothing in this book is complicated. There may be nothing new in this book for you. There may be things you have tried and dismissed. There may be things you don't want to try as you don't believe in them. There may be things you would like to try but don't feel that you have the energy/money/time. You *must* be committed of course. I am not trying to be condescending in any way, but I can only speak from my own experience when I say that it took me a good while before I was fully **ready** to be committed. I always had an excuse as to why I wouldn't try something, or (more likely) why I was giving up on something I had tried which hadn't given me the results I wanted within a set (quite often) short period of time.

For me, I had to go *all in*. Once I signed up for the online M.E. course, I somehow knew that this was it. No excuses. No giving up. No half-hearted attempts. No cheating. No waiting for the quick fix. No hoping that someone else would come along and 'fix' me. I was determined to give it my all for six full months. At the start, this seemed like a really long time! Looking back, I know it genuinely wasn't! I could have six months of excuses... or six months of progress. I am delighted that I chose progress. Genuinely, I didn't expect to see **so** much progress in that time, and even now I still can't always believe how well I did in my recovery.

The biggest turning point for me came when I started to have faith in myself. I told myself that I **could**, and I **would** recover. I didn't just say it though (well, at times I did), I worked on myself to such an extent that I began to fully *believe* it. I believed in myself. And I believe in **you**. I believe that you **can** recover. If you are reading this to try and gain a better understanding of someone you love who has this horrible illness (and again, I thank you for doing that), I believe that they can heal. It won't be easy. It won't be overnight. It may not be in six months, or even a year, or even two years. In one year I recovered a huge amount, but I knew there was still a way to get to where I wanted to be and to be doing the things I wanted to be doing. I'm excited about my future. I can't wait to see where I am this time next year as I genuinely believe that I will only go from strength to strength. I have my future goals set out. I have my plans and I know the steps that I need to take to get to where I want to be. My recent ear infection at the time of writing this section has been a bit of a blessing, as it has reminded me that I need to continue the work I do on myself every single day. While I don't take things for granted any more, I also appreciate that it can be easy to start to forget how bad things were and start to forge ahead a bit more quickly than my body would like. I must remember where I was and how far I have come. While I don't ever want to live in fear, I also don't ever want to push myself so that I risk being ill again.

I will be grateful for every morning I wake up pain and symptom free. I will continue to nourish my body with healthy, nutritious foods. I will practice mindfulness in the activities I do and incorporate meditation into each day. I will practice the physical activities each day which keep my body fit and healthy, without ever pushing my body in a way which may set it back. I will choose what I fill my mind with, choosing positive things which uplift me and make me feel good. I will spend times with the ones I love. I will ask for support when I need it and accept help when it is offered. I will keep saying no to things which don't support the way of life I am choosing. I will keep learning about new things and remain open to the fact that there may be better ways to do some of the things I am doing now and be willing to make changes if there is a chance that they may help me in any way. I will read books and listen to audios which aid my recovery. I will seek out like-minded people in my life who support me and help me know that I am on the right path for me. I will get outside every day. I will continue with activities and treatments which help my body heal effectively. I will listen to my body and do my best to give it what it needs. I will work on myself so that I am as strong as possible in both my body and my mind. I will do my utmost to remove myself from any situations which bring too much negativity into my world. I will remember that I have been ill... but I will also remember that I have recovered – and that I did it myself!

None of this is complicated – but of course that does not mean that any of it is **easy**. I know that I only get this one body, and this one life. I became ill during a period of my life, and I have learned lessons from that illness. I know to never take my body, or life, for granted and I know to be grateful for the things that I **do** have, rather than always focusing on the things I do not have.

M.E. AND OTHER PEOPLE

I am well aware of how hard it has been for not only me suffering with the devastating consequences of this illness, but also the people closest to me. My immediate family lived every day with me, watching me struggle. In a lot of ways, they were quite helpless about being able to do much about it. Yes, of course they were able to support and help me, but they couldn't do anything to cure me. To watch someone you love being in such an horrendous condition is really awful. As a mum, I know what it's like when my kids get ill, and I wish I could take it away from them. Thankfully, my children haven't had any physical illness which has ever lasted for more than a few days, so I have always been able to be logical about it and know that a few days of extra cuddles and love will help ease their suffering, and before too long they will be back to normal. But what about when a few days won't fix anything? What about when you have to wake each day and wonder how your loved one will be today? Will it be a bed-bound day? Will you watch your loved one putting on a brave face, even though you can see everything is hurting them so much? Will you have to bury your own feelings of fear and even your own tiredness because you are so concerned about not adding any additional pressure on them? Will your needs have to take a back seat because you are so busy trying to make things as comfortable as possible for someone else? Will your own already heavy workload be added to because your loved one quite simply can't do anything due to illness?

It is so, so difficult! I truly don't think people are aware of how hard it is for the family and supporters of an ill person. The effects are so strong and whole lives can be turned upside down, even for people who aren't physically ill themselves.

I could see that it was having detrimental effects on my family through my own illness, and that made it even harder for me. It made me want to pretend I was better than I was because I hated them being upset over me. It made me conscious of the things that I couldn't do and the pressures I was adding to my family and friends. It made me feel so guilty about being ill. Guilt can be an awful emotion, and I don't think it serves us any purpose with regards to this illness. A build-up of guilt is totally toxic to a body which is already so overwhelmed.

I faced M.E. during the Covid pandemic, which meant that much of it was spent during lockdown. This had huge impacts on us all as a family as we were all in the house together... all the time. There was no way I could put a brave face on for that long and so my husband and children saw things which I had been able to hide when they went out to work and school. My children saw me fall over, be unable to make it up the stairs on my own or have to put my head down on the table during mealtimes because I was just too exhausted to even sit and eat properly. They heard me wincing in pain and even crying out at times when I was struggling so much that I just couldn't hold it in anymore. They saw how often I needed to stop what I was doing because I didn't have the energy to carry on.

Children who have family members who are unwell really feel it too. To me, it is so important that this is taken into consideration, and they are able to get support too. It is vital that they have other family members, friends, teachers and even professionals who they can speak to openly about their feelings, as the last thing we would want would be for them to spend years suppressing emotions. Obviously in our case, everyone at the children's school knew about our situation as I had been working there and stayed in close contact with lots of the staff during my illness, so that made it a bit easier. I would certainly recommend that schoolteachers and even extra-curricular activity teachers are made aware of what is going on, so that children know they have a safe person to talk to if they ever feel the need to. Although it may seem like you are sharing very private information and it may feel uncomfortable, this really can have a big impact on children's mental and emotional health and so it is good to have as much all-round support as possible, for everyone involved.

When you are supporting someone through illness, you may often feel helpless. It can be hard knowing what the right thing to do, and even say is. While some days a person with M.E. can seem to be quite 'normal' (I hate to use that word as I know there is no such thing as 'normal', but I think most people will understand what I mean when I say this and it is in no way meant disrespectfully), other days may be truly horrific... and quite often there is no way of telling what each day will bring. Even when you start off having quite a 'good' day, things can change by the hour. You may wake up feeling ok, and then by lunchtime be in so much pain and be so fatigued that you can't even string a sentence together. Making plans can be hard and it may feel like everyone's life is on hold as you never know whether you will be able to make it to something.

One of the best things you can do to support someone with such an illness, is to simply believe them. This sounds almost ridiculous to say, but it is amazing how many people still question the authenticity of this illness. I think that unless you are living with someone and seeing the changes, it can be hard to grasp that someone can be **that** ill with often no clear explanation as to why they are like that. When even the medical profession can query the genuineness of it, I can see why so many other people may question it. It is important that people know that this is a **real** condition and that it is not something else. M.E. it is a stand-alone illness and should never be treated the same as any other illness, such as depression.

I remember being paranoid that people would think I was lazy. I had always worked hard, and I was so conscious about what people thought of me that this really bothered me. While we all know that it shouldn't matter what other people think, it can take a lot of mindset work to not really worry about it (thankfully I'm much less bothered now, but it took time and effort!) I even occasionally worried that James would think I was lazy, even though he could see how physically and mentally hard everything suddenly was for me, and so I ended up pushing myself at home when I really shouldn't have done. It is important that if you are supporting someone, that you do let them know that you **know** that they are not being lazy. Again, it may sound daft or simple, but it is such a huge help when people you love tell you such supportive things. When you are feeling like you may be pathetic, or a failure, or weak... sometimes someone reminding you that you are none of these things, and that what you are, is in fact **ill**, can make a big difference!

People who are unwell need help in so many ways, but may often be too proud, or scared to ask for it. It can be a big challenge asking for or accepting help. We live in a society now where many of us may like to be seen to help others, but we aren't always great at accepting help ourselves. Plus, a lot of people who get ill with M.E. may be the type of people who have always been the helpers themselves. Which means they may expect to have a lot of people willing to return that help, but sadly this isn't always the case. If you know someone who is ill and are able to help them in any way, even if you are not a direct supporter of them, then please do always consider offering your help. If it is refused, offer again and again. Let the person know that you want to help as you want them to recover to the best of their ability. I remember my lovely friend Carrie turning up one day with a cottage pie she had made for us all. I had such mixed emotions about it. One part of me felt like a failure accepting food cooked for us, while another part was so grateful that I didn't have to try to cook that evening or ask James to. I realised that it was my pride getting in the way and that was an issue I would have to deal with. Ironically, if my friend had offered to cook for me, I would have most probably said no, so her turning up unannounced with it was just wonderful. We were all grateful to have a delicious, home-cooked meal that night. On another occasion, my friend Adele came over and had to help me get dressed as I simply couldn't manage it that day.

M.E. is a difficult illness to get your head around and so if you are supporting someone through it, or even supporting someone who is supporting a loved one through it, I would recommend gaining an understanding of it. Obviously, this book is a great start and if you are reading this to try and help someone you know, then may I take a minute to personally thank you. You are incredible to be helping someone and I know it will be very tough for you. I recall speaking to a lady one day when I was working in The Sanctuary. We got chatting and she told me that her daughter was there for a treatment as she had M.E. I told her about my story, and she was quite overwhelmed as she said that she had never actually talked to anyone else with M.E. She was a lovely lady who obviously wanted to do the best for her daughter... and she felt helpless. She worried about what she could be doing to help, and she felt like she was saying the wrong thing sometimes. I realised again how hard it is for people supporting loved ones who are ill.

It is certainly worth reading information from reputable sites such as ME Action.

If you can go to doctor's appointments with your loved one, then that is always beneficial. Being in a doctor's when you are unwell can often be very overwhelming. Trying to focus enough to explain what is going on is absolutely exhausting and you can forget to mention important things. It is also **really** hard to listen to, understand and actually remember what the doctor is saying to you. Just the effort of listening after the effort of getting yourself to the appointment is likely to be so very difficult, so to have someone there to help you with that is brilliant. My mother-in-law Cathy came with me to see the M.E. specialist and it helped me (and her) so much. She was able to take in information that I simply couldn't and could then relay it to me when I wasn't quite as exhausted, as well as relaying things to my husband. I remember the specialist telling me one thing but when I told James what she had said, Cathy was able to (very kindly) correct me. I simply hadn't understood what I was being told due to the level of exhaustion I was in. I am so grateful that she was able to do that (on top of everything else she was doing to help me and the rest of the family).

One extra bit of advice I would give to anyone helping to support someone, is to not forget to look after yourself! When you effectively become a carer, it can be easy to let your own self-care slip. It is absolutely *essential* that you care for yourself properly. You *cannot* look after someone else to the best of your ability if you end up struggling with your own health, so it isn't selfish in any way when you take time out for yourself. It can be mentally and physically exhausting being a carer. Not only are you having to deal with your own life, but you are also having to take on extra responsibilities. Seeing someone you love become so ill can have major implications for you and you may feel that you don't want to burden your loved ones with any of your own worries. You may, of course, be worried about whether your loved one will ever get better. All these extra issues can take its toll on you over time. I would certainly recommend that you accept help yourself. It may be hard for your loved one to accept help, and they may not want outside people coming in to help, but it's important that they realise that **you** need support too. It is also worth considering speaking to someone. Bottling up emotions and worries does nobody any good and with something as serious and life changing as this, you must really consider what it may be doing to your own emotional health. Please don't ever feel that you must cope alone. Ask for, and accept, as much help and support as you can. You are doing a wonderful thing helping your loved one... and you are very important! Please realise that you are never alone and recognise that your own emotions about what is going on are validated. It is never just one person who is affected when some gets ill.

ACKNOWLEDGEMENTS

My faves... my world... my everything... James, Jack & Isobel. Even I am struggling to put into words what you guys mean to me. I will forever be beyond grateful for you all. You stood, sat & lay by my side throughout all of this... and now you get to walk, run, swim, ski, climb & dance with me. You have all been incredible and I can never thank you enough for all you have done. You have been my reason for working so hard to create this wonderful life I live. Thank you for believing in me. Thank you for giving me strength when I didn't think I had any. Thank you for simply being yourselves... all of you are so much more than enough exactly as you are.

James... soul mate doesn't even come close. My most favourite human being. I'm delighted that we can return to planning our future the way we wanted to. I'm so proud of you for all you have achieved and are going on to achieve. You're the best.

Jack... you saw so much & while sometimes that still hurts my heart, I know that the type of man you will grow into will be shaped by this & you will have the most empathy for others. You make me so proud every day with your caring soul & your hard work. You shine my love, you truly do. Believe in yourself the way I believe in you, and you will be unstoppable. My favourite boy!

Isobel... the world needs more of you! A wonderful mixture of kindness & firecrackerness! Your strength and determination are second to none and I already know that you will achieve whatever you desire. You have also learned so much along this journey and I know you will give that back to others. I'm so proud of you. Keep being you & make the world a stronger place. My favourite girl.

Chewy... you brought me light when I was struggling to find it. You were meant for me.

Mum and dad... thank you for everything. Always my biggest cheerleaders and supporters. Thank you for all the help you have given to Team Pod along the way. We all appreciate it so much and we love you so much. You showed me the meaning of unconditional love growing up, and I'm so glad that it's never gone away. It means the world to me. I love you both so much.

Cathy... my Mily. Thank you for everything you have done for me, and for all of us. You went above and beyond in helping me recover and I will be forever grateful. I am honoured that I get to look after your boy and your grand babies... thank you for helping me do that! Mily, friend and so much more... I love you.

Stevie... keep being you! You make all of us smile and have brought so much to our family. Thank you! Love you (mate!).

Michel and Debbie... thank you for your ongoing support and love. You have both been incredible to me personally, and to the rest of our Team Pod. I appreciate everything you have done for us and know that I would never have recovered to this level without you guys being there for us in the many ways you have been. You are both so fantastic and I couldn't love you more than I do!

Chris... I love you so much mate and I'm beyond proud of you and how you inspire others through your honesty and integrity. You shine far brighter than you may ever realise.

Jo and Ben... thank you for all of your help and support... and your promise to Team Pod (although obviously we don't want to take you up on it!!). Knowing that you are always there for all of us, for literally anything, has meant, and still means, the world to me (and all of us). We love you so much.

Steph, Debs, Tracey, Naomi, Carrie, Kris & Adele... thank you for sticking with me while the old me had to change, & still being here for the new me.

To my Sanctuary family... I literally love you all so much. I cannot imagine how much longer this journey would have taken without finding you. Thank you for helping me find my way and encouraging me to do the things I needed to do. Thank for you holding my hand when I hobbled upstairs and believing that one day I would throw away my walking stick. Thank you for giving me faith that I could do this and showing me the way. Thank you for taking a chance on me when nobody else would have. Thank you for allowing me to be me, you make me shine brighter than I ever have done, and you help me be happy to be me! If only everyone in the world could spend time here with us, I'm convinced the world would be the place we all want it to be!

Ness, Tony, Malcolm, Sue, Sue, Nicola, Lee, Roger, Michelle, Fiona, Julie, Nikki, Trish, Lou, Rob, Lissa, Charlotte, V, Jilly, Chris... you are all amazing.

V, Stina, & David... Thank you for being such huge reasons for me getting better!

Alex... thank you for giving me the push I needed, a world of encouragement along the way, & for always being in my corner. I will always be grateful for you.

My Y-Family... thank you for all of your love and support over the years. Your friendships have meant so much to me and you all helped me go through some of my darkest days with love and much needed humour! I appreciate every single one of you in different ways and will always be thankful for the ways you showed up for me.

To everyone who has played a part, no matter how big or small, in helping me on this journey... I thank you from the bottom of my heart. I am so honoured that actually, there are **so** many people who I could credit with helping me in some way, that I could write another book! I will choose not to do that of course... but I hope that if you are taking the time to read this and you know that you have been part of my life, that you **know** how grateful I am to you, and why!! There have been so many people who have said a kind word, encouraged me, cheered me on and supported me... it's truly incredible! Thank you to everyone who has been rooting for my recovery, whether silently or vocally... that support went out into the universe and **did** reach me, whether you believe that or not! So thank you!

Naomi & Amy – thank you for all your help and support with the editing! I appreciate it so much!

To Karen... as in - to ME... thank you!! Thank you for committing to yourself. Thank you for wanting to get better **so** badly that you were willing to do *whatever* it took. Thank you for not giving up, even when it seemed things weren't working. Thank you for doing the work, for allowing the healing even when it was messy, and even painful, at times. Thank you for putting yourself first, even when your ego told you that it was a selfish thing to do. Thank you for believing that by putting the work in you would be the person you dreamed of being. Thank you for writing this book, knowing that there will be people who may mock it/you, but knowing that if you can help just ONE person, it will all have been worth it. Thank you for being ill, so that you could help others see that choice is so important in life, and so that you could show others how recovery IS possible. Thank you for putting yourself out there, even when others disagreed with what you were doing... so that you could help others on a similar path to you. Thank you for having the gall to write yourself into the acknowledgments, even though others may think it is weird... to show that self-love is not just words I say, but a life I truly believe in and follow.

SUMMARY OF MY RECOVERY 'PLAN'

Work on my mindset daily to keep it healthy and positive.

Remember that my recovery is now my full-time 'job'.

Feed my body with nutritious food. (If it grows, eat it. If it contains chemicals, forget it.)

Take my supplements.

Do some gentle movement, do it with purpose, congratulate myself when I have done it and do *not* over-do it!

Do whatever helps to ease my symptoms and be willing to try 'alternatives'.

Pace my activities every day.

Rest! Rest properly! No distractions.

Sleep!

Complete the M.E. course and do everything suggested.

Attend counselling/therapy sessions.

Meditate. Every day. More than once if possible. Practice mindfulness too.

Say/think positive affirmations every day, as many times as I can. When a negative thought enters, send it away with a positive affirmation.

Practice self-care and ensure I am a priority and not a last thought.

Cut down/remove my social media, watching the TV and accessing the news.

Get support from positive support groups. Don't get caught up in complaining!

Listen to my body. It wants to keep me safe and its having to resort to all of this pain because I refused to listen for too long. Do as it tells me.

Stop comparing myself to anyone else – either those I perceive to be better than me, or those I believe to be worse than me.

Work on myself! Know that I am worth it! Practice gratitude. Have faith that I WILL RECOVER!

MY LAST PIECE OF ADVICE

I have written this book in the hope that it helps people. I especially want it to help people with M.E., fibromyalgia or Long Covid. However, I would love it to even help people without these conditions! I told myself that all the work I put into this book would be totally worth it if it helped even one person.

Here's the thing though. I can't actually help you... I can only help to encourage you to *help yourself*! I can't do any of the things I talk about in here for you; I can only let you know that the things I've written about helped me, and I believe that they could help you too! But you must put the work in.

I'm not meaning to sound harsh or judgmental here. Everything I have written in this book comes from my heart and with love for everyone going through this horrible chapter in their lives. (And I really believe it's a chapter... not the end of your book!) I've lived through the pain of M.E. I know what it's like to wake every day scared, angry, bitter, feeling useless and unable to look into the future without worry and fear. I've told myself that this is probably as good as it gets. I've believed that I would never get better. I've cried because I've got worse. I've wanted to wait for a doctor to offer me a cure or an effective treatment. I struggled to have faith in myself.

But I *have* got better! I've got better because of all of the things I've done in here. I've recovered because I stopped waiting for a doctor to 'fix' me. I took my recovery into my own hands, and I've left M.E. behind me.

I STOPPED MAKING EXCUSES!

This will be blunt (and in all honesty, I struggle with bluntness because I get concerned about offending people, but I feel it needs to be said) ...

YOU HAVE TO STOP MAKING EXCUSES!

There, I said it. I truly don't mean to offend; but if you are offended, then there may be a reason for that. Guess what... I used to get offended when anyone suggested something new to try and I would tell them/myself "Oh I've tried EVERYTHING!" But the truth was, I hadn't. I hadn't sorted my mindset out! I was telling myself that it was ok for someone else, but it wasn't for me.

Notice when you have read through this book whether you have been making excuses/throwing up reasons why this *won't* work for *you*. You may tell yourself you have given something a try and it didn't work. You may believe that it's 'ok for her' because she has more support/money/time/available resources; that she hasn't been as ill as me, or for as long as I have. You may have a lot of self-doubt, because you've been *so* unwell for *so* long and you just can't see a way through it. You may assume that if the doctors can't cure you, you must be 'incurable'.

Let me tell you something... I have said/thought all these things. I read/heard people's recovery stories and I told myself it was ok for them. I had to realise that I was giving myself permission to stay ill. I was making excuses. I was staying trapped in my own victim story.

For me to get better I had to really work on my mindset. Rather than looking at someone who had recovered and feeling like that couldn't happen to me because of any number of reasons, I chose to look at them and *learn* from them. I wanted to know what they had done to improve themselves. I had to be willing to try **everything**, no matter how 'woo-woo' or tough it sounded. I had to commit to doing everything for a good amount of time. I had to be consistent, and I had to truly BELIEVE that it would work. Every time a negative thought popped in my head, where I told myself that something wasn't working, I had to replace it with a helpful thought. I would change my thoughts by repeating positive affirmations. I wanted every cell in my body to tingle with self-belief. I knew that other people had gotten better... so there was my ***proof*** that it was possible! I had to take that proof and apply it to my own belief that **I** too could recover.

With all of my heart, I want **you** to recover, and I want you to live a wonderful life. I want you to *never* again take anything for granted! I want you to be able to look back at the time you were ill and realise that it was, indeed, a *chapter* in your life, rather than the whole book. I want you to learn to **listen** to your body, so that you know when it is telling you something in order to keep you safe... and I want you to do what your body says so that you keep healthy.

You don't have to focus on the people who don't get better... and you don't have to be one of them! There are people recovering from M.E. every day... *you* can be one of those! You truly can.

I hope that in six months from now you will be well on your way to recovery. I know that when you fully commit to your recovery, it IS possible.

I wish you the best of luck and I pray that you have been able to find even one thing in here which will help you on your own personal journey.

Thank you for taking the time to read this. As I have just said, I want this book to help at least one person. To tell the truth, it already has. Writing this helped ME. It reminds me of the things that I need to keep doing, and it reminds me of my 'WHY' - why I needed to recover. Find *your* why my friend, it makes all the difference.

Sending love and strength to you. My last words are to remind you of the affirmations I used to help me get through this (you can even sing it, I am doing!) ... "I am happy, I am healthy, all is well."

SUGGESTED BOOK LIST

I read or listen to a book every single day. Of course, that can be difficult to do when you have M.E. and cognitive functioning is hard! However, there are some books I would absolutely recommend you read in your own recovery journey. If you are able to read then that's wonderful... if not, then I can fully recommend listening to the audio book version!

MINDSET BOOKS....

Heal your life - Louise Hay

I ♥□ Me - David Hamilton

Happy Mind, Happy Life - Dr Rangan Chatterjee

Loving What is - Byron Katie

The Secret - Rhonda Byrne

Don't sweat the small stuff - Richard Carlson

How to heal yourself when no one else can - Amy B. Scher

Feel the fear & do it anyway - Susan Jeffers

Life loves you - Robert Holden & Louise Hay

The universe has your back - Gabrielle Bernstein

The power of now - Eckhart Tolle

Ask & it is given - (Abraham) Esther & Jerry Hicks

A return to Love - Marianne Williamson

Mindfulness for health – Vidyamala Burch & Danny Penman

M.E. SPECIFIC BOOKS....

Recovery From CFS – 50 Recovery stories – edited & complied by Alexandra Barton

CFS Unravelled – Dan Neuffer

Diagnosis and treatment of CFS & ME – Dr Sarah Myhill

Decode your fatigue – Alex Howard

Call For Soulwork – Gretchen Brooks Nassar

From fatigued to fantastic – Jacob Teiterbaum

CFS/ME – Support for family & friends – Elizabeth Turp

Exhausted – Nick Polizzi & Pedram Shojai (not M.E. specific but very good)

FOOD BOOKS....

Eat. Nourish. Glow – Amelia Freer

The grain-free, sugar-free, dairy-free cookbook – Leah Webb

Deliciously Ella – Ella Woodward

The Grain Brain – Dr David Perlmutter

Salt, Sugar, Fat – Michael Moss

Good sugar, bad sugar – Allen Carr